T0170062

ONCE WELL BELOVED

ONCE WELL BELOVED

Remembering a British Columbia Great War Sacrifice

Michael Sasges

ROYAL BC MUSEUM

VICTORIA

Once Well Beloved
Remembering a British Columbia Great War Sacrifice

Copyright © 2019 by Michael Sasges

Published by the Royal BC Museum, 675 Belleville Street,
Victoria, British Columbia, V8W 9W2, Canada.

The Royal BC Museum is located on the traditional territories of the
Lekwungen (Songhees and Xwsepsum Nations). We extend our
appreciation for the opportunity to live and learn on this territory.

All rights reserved. No part of this book may be reproduced or transmitted in
any form by any means without permission in writing from the publisher,
except by a reviewer, who may quote brief passages in a review.

Front cover photo Nicola Valley Museum Archives Association PAS201
Back cover photo © Merritt Herald / Cole Wagner, 2016
Cover, interior design and typesetting by Jeff Werner
Index by Stephen Ullstrom

Library and Archives Canada Cataloguing in Publication
Title: Once well beloved : remembering a British Columbia Great War sacrifice /
Michael Sasges.
Names: Sasges, Michael, 1952- author. | Royal British Columbia Museum, publisher.
Description: Includes bibliographical references and index.
Identifiers: Canadiana (print) 20190152184 | Canadiana (ebook) 20190152230
| ISBN 9780772672551 (softcover) | ISBN 9780772672995 (EPUB)
| ISBN 9780772673008 (Kindle) | ISBN 9780772673015 (PDF)
Subjects: LCSH: World War, 1914-1918—British Columbia—Nicola River Valley.
| LCSH: Soldiers—British Columbia—Nicola River Valley—Biography.
Classification: LCC FC3845.N52 S27 2019 | DDC 971.1/72—dc23

21 20 19   1 2 3 4 5 6 7 8 9 10

Printed and bound in Canada by Friesens.

To the grandchildren

Contents

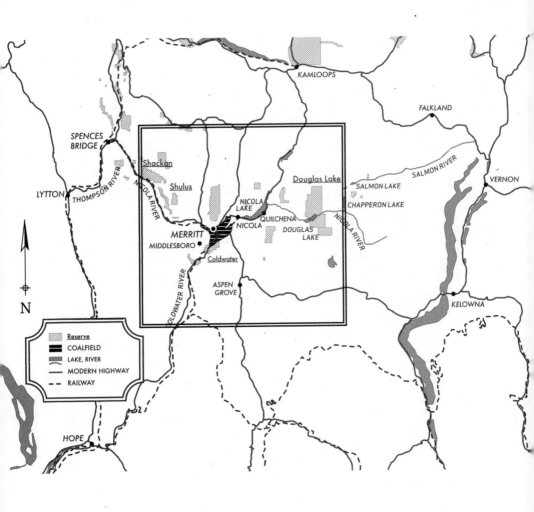

KAMLOOPS

FALKLAND

SPENCES
BRIDGE

Shackan

Shulus

Douglas Lake

SALMON RIVER

VERNON

LYTTON

THOMPSON RIVER

NICOLA RIVER

Nicola
Lake

NICOLA
LAKE

SALMON LAKE

CHAPPERON LAKE

QUILCHENA

NICOLA

DOUGLAS
LAKE

NICOLA RIVER

MERRITT

MIDDLESBORO

Coldwater

COLDWATER RIVER

ASPEN
GROVE

KELOWNA

N

Reserve
COALFIELD
LAKE, RIVER
MODERN HIGHWAY
RAILWAY

HOPE

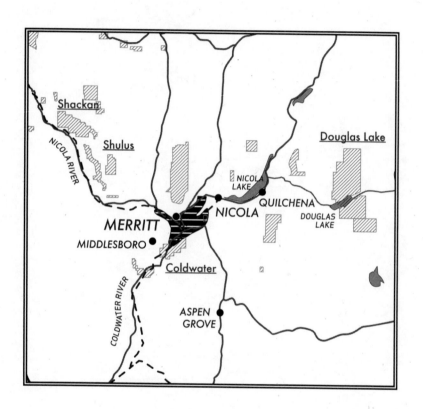

Introduction: "Where Is Merritt?"

A granite cenotaph has stood in the British Columbia town of Merritt since 1921. On three of its faces are inscribed the names of 44 Nicola Valley men who died soldiering in the First World War. On the fourth face is inscribed the dedication. The men are "our well beloved dead who died that we might live." Twelve of the 44 are remembered on the pages that follow.[1] Their circumstances of death recommended 10 of them for investigation. They are the three who died first, in 1915; the four who died at Vimy, in 1917; and the three who died last, in 1918 and '19. Their circumstances in life recommend the other two. One was a voluntary exile, from family dissolution in England. The second was an involuntary exile from family *and* community dissolution in British Columbia.

To recall the "well beloved" and those who knew them or knew of them is to recall the British Columbia of the first two decades of the twentieth century. They and their

The first Nicola Valley men to volunteer for Great War military
service left Merritt by train on August 15, 18 and 19, 1914. Great
Britain had declared war on August 4.

Nicola Valley Museum & Archives PAS201.

contemporaries were consequential British Columbians. They were both the cause and the consequence of the industrialization and urbanization, and the government deliberations and decisions, that occurred in those decades in the province. The communities they peopled and the corridors built between them sustain many of us who make our homes in British Columbia today.[2]

Those two decades also enthrall us today. All that occurred was done without benefit of treaty. Indeed, all was done as the Indigenous peoples in the province were asking the Dominion government to acknowledge title and initiate treaty negotiations. Nicola Valley men were prominent organizers and leaders in the agitations that occurred.

The Nicola Valley is located in British Columbia's southern Interior. It is an aberration and an anomaly, a small part of the smallest of British Columbia's 14 geographical zones. The bunchgrass ecological zone covers less than 1 per cent of the province's landmass. Lying in the rain shadow of the Coast Mountains and the North Cascades, the bunchgrass zone is famously hot and dry.

The Nicola River is a tributary's tributary. Its principal is the Thompson, a Fraser River tributary. The Nicola joins the Thompson at Spences Bridge, and the Thompson joins the Fraser at Lytton, 35 kilometres below Spences Bridge. The Nicola is a relatively diminutive watercourse. The Fraser River is about 1,400 kilometres long. The Thompson is about 500 kilometres, and the Nicola, about 200. It rises about 1,600 metres above sea level and empties into the Thompson at 225 metres above sea level. The confluence elevation is misleading.

Elevations of 1,000 metres are a few kilometres away, and elevations of 1,500 metres a few kilometres from those.

Any number of lost-seagull distances permit relative positioning of the valley. A physical-geography distance is this: the Nicola River rises about 290 kilometres north and east of the Fraser River's mouth on the Strait of Georgia. A cultural-geography distance is this: Merritt is about 210 kilometres north and east of Vancouver.[3]

Humankind has probably continuously inhabited the Nicola Valley for about 4,000 years. By the First World War, the Syilx people of the upper valley and the Nlaka'pamux people of the lower valley sustained themselves by foraging, by herding and cultivating, and by wage labour. They hunted, fished and harvested roots and berries. They worked with livestock, for themselves and for hire, and cultivated hay, fruit and vegetables for sale and barter. The first horses arrived on the southern Interior Plateau in the first half of the eighteenth century, and the first cattle in the first half of the nineteenth.[4] A woman who lived in the valley as a girl and young woman, from 1911 to 1926, recalled "Native Indians from Merritt [selling] vegetables from horse and wagon."[5] Indigenous labourers also worked for wages, as cowboys and loggers and navvies and teamsters. By the Great War, between 600 and 700 men, women and children lived on the 24 reserves above and below the confluence of the Nicola and Coldwater rivers.

Approximate comparisons with the pre-colonial Indigenous population in the valley exist. In 1868, the colonial civil servant who imposed the first reserves on the Indigenous peoples of the valley counted 250 men, women and children attached to two chiefs. Because the count was conducted in the summer, many people were away from the valley, including one of the chiefs. Five years earlier, smallpox had devastated the Indigenous peoples of the Fraser and Thompson country. In the last decade of the nineteenth century, James Teit recorded this Nlaka'pamux memory:

> *The old people say that forty or fifty years ago, when travelling along [the] Thompson River, the smoke of Indian camp-fires was always in view. This will be better understood when it is noted that the course of [the] Thompson is very tortuous, and that in many places one can see but a very short distance up or down the river. The old Indians compare the number of people formerly living in the vicinity of Lytton to "ants about an ant-hill."[6]*

The first enumeration of settlers was conducted in 1875, a year after British Columbia entered Confederation. There were 40 men eligible to vote in the new province's Yale electoral district. By "profession, trade or calling," all but three were farmers. The exceptions were a blacksmith, a millwright or machinist, and a flour miller. There were women and children, too. A commercial directory recorded their presence this way: "Population of Nicola District up to December 31st 1876. White male adults, 55; white female adults, 24; white children, 40; Mexican male adults, 8; half-breed children, 24. Total population bona fide residents, 151."[7] The Mexicans were packers who wintered their stock in the valley, and had done so since before the arrival of the first settlers. But the count underrepresents: it excludes the Indigenous mothers of the "half-breed children."

The last nineteenth-century count of valley voters occurred in 1898. At least 120 Nicola Valley men were eligible to vote in the electoral district's west and north ridings.[8] There are no commercial directories extant that record the total contemporaneous settler population, but the 1901 census of Canada provides a good count. Two enumerators counted almost 300 settler men, women and children in a region extending from the mouth of the Nicola River (probably) to Douglas Lake (certainly). Only the inclusion of two names, those of Joseph Coutlee and Joseph Greaves, demonstrates that the enumerator for Yale North counted people living above the mouth of Nicola Lake. Greaves was a founding partner of the Douglas Lake cattle syndicate, today Canada's largest ranch. Coutlee was the ranch's head cowboy for more than 50 years.

After doubling in the last 25 years of the nineteenth century, although not from and not to much, the settler population more than quadrupled in the first 10 years of the twentieth. The 1911 census of Canada enumerator counted more than 1,300 settlers in roughly the same area. Industrial exploitation of the coal measures found near the confluence of the Coldwater and Nicola rivers, long anticipated and quickly realized, drove the boom.[9] "Where is Merritt, asked a Vancouver [man] of a Merritt man a few days ago," the *Merritt Herald and Nicola Valley Advocate* editorialized in 1913. "We must not pity the Vancouverite's ignorance but recollect that six years ago where our city now stands was but a hayfield."[10]

Two railwaymen organized the industrialization of the valley. Miners, mostly from the coalfields of the United Kingdom, did the heavy lifting. Thomas Shaughnessy, president of the Canadian Pacific Railway, ordered a short line built between the CPR mainline at Spences Bridge and the Merritt Coalfield, hoping to relieve the railway's reliance on Vancouver Island coal. The line was built in 1906 by as many as 1,500 men. That same year John Hendry, a Vancouver industrialist, incorporated Nicola Valley Coal & Coke to buy up coal properties in the valley. Hendry was Great Northern's Canadian representative, the legendary railway capitalist J. J. Hill's man in Canada.[11] He had been investigating opportunities in the Merritt Coalfield for at least five years. He anticipated immediate revenue from the CPR, eventual sales to the urbanized Lower Mainland, and an opportunity to supply the smelters and railways of southeast British Columbia as soon as Great Northern had completed its line between Winnipeg and Vancouver. Hendry's Middlesboro colliery started shipping in 1907.[12] In 1912, its fifth full year of production, the colliery employed more than 300 men and boys, and three other valley collieries employed 100 more.[13]

The settlers of this rapidly industrializing valley built the valley recognizable today. In 1911, they requested and received a local-government charter from the provincial legislature. They lit up the night: the "City" of Merritt owned the electrical plant. They organized a public-safety agency, the Merritt Volunteer Fire Department. They built churches and clubrooms.[14] They taught and learned about mine safety and farming, practised their religious faiths and exercised military skills. Boer War veterans among them started a militia, the

Members of the first Nicola Valley Coal & Coke mine rescue squad gathered in front of their employer's office in the pithead settlement of Middlesboro in 1912. The occasion is probably the issuance, by the provincial government, of certificates of competency. The man in the cloth cap at the office door is Matthew Dover Ovington, grandfather of the late Larry Ovington, from whom this photograph comes.

Gail and Larry Ovington Collection.

grandly caparisoned 31st Regiment, British Columbia Horse. They published and read three weekly newspapers. They were a gregarious people. The record of their dances and smokers and concerts, their lectures and athletic competitions, still delights a century later.

The search for a break from the working day was not the sole motivation for their socializing. They danced the night away because they could not improve their communal circumstances without the proceeds of their gatherings. There was no fire brigade until there had been a dance. The first weekly meeting of the fire department for which there are minutes puts the relationship between socializing and civic improvement this way: "Report was read, of committee appointed at public meeting to hold a dance for the purpose of raising funds to organize a Fire Brigade. Dance being held on May 29th [1911]."[15]

The valley's newspapers, the small merchant community and the religious organizations passed much time acknowledging and negotiating the advance of Merritt toward "hub" status, and the retreat of agrarian Nicola, at the mouth of Nicola Lake. "Coal made Merritt go until after the start of the Second World War," a collection of settler reminiscences observes. Coal also made Nicola go away. "Coal started Merritt; otherwise Nicola may ... have remained as the centre [of the valley]," the late Allan Collett, longtime mayor of Merritt, once commented.[16] When the 31st BC Horse was formed in 1910, the banquet was held in Nicola, but subsequent banquets were in Merritt. When the Methodist lay leadership met, they tried to avoid meeting in the same community consecutively. They might meet in a private residence in Middlesboro in one quarter, for example, and in lower Nicola in the next. They maintained two Sunday schools, and their ministers held two Sunday services.[17]

Industrialization of the Nicola Valley created another reversal of fortunes. Before the railway, Indigenous people were the majority population in the valley. After the railway, they were the minority. The original population probably outnumbered the recently arrived at least two to one in 1901, the year of the fourth census of Canada. The recently arrived probably outnumbered the original population 10 years later. Precise Indigenous numbers are unknown. The Indigenous people of the valley were enumerated in 1901, but the returns no longer exist. They were not enumerated in 1911. Their Indian Agent quit before he counted the residents of valley's reserves. The Department of Indian Affairs published Indigenous population estimates in its annual reports, however. They are 662 in 1901/1902 and 656 in 1911/12.

The demographic reversal was of enormous consequence for the valley's Indigenous residents. Surveillance, for example, intensified. Before the railway, the residents of the Indigenous settlements endured scrutiny by Indian Agent and missionary, usually from a distance. After the railway, the residents of Indigenous settlements also had to endure surveillance by game wardens assigned to the valley by the provincial government in response to settler complaints about Indigenous foraging. Before the railway, there was no local-government authority with bylaws that Indigenous people might infringe, intentionally or not. After the railway, there was the city of Merritt. The railway also brought an additional provincial police constable. There was one at Nicola, as there had been since the 1870s, and one at Merritt. One or two city of Merritt constables policed the town. Before the railway, Indigenous residents of the lower valley controlled the transportation of goods between the Nicola and Similkameen valleys, or between Spences Bridge and Princeton. ("Some of them can turn out as fine a four-horse freight team as can be seen anywhere," their Indian Agent wrote in his annual report for 1901/1902.[18]) The railway eventually eliminated this work. ("Freighting has declined greatly since completion of the Nicola railway," their agent wrote in his annual report for 1909/1910.[19])

Remarkably, three organizers of the Indigenous lands-and-rights agitations that occurred in the first decades of the twentieth century resided in the Nicola Valley or nearby. They and the people they represented were the first Indigenous groups in the Fraser and Thompson drainages to experience the resumption of railway construction after the completion of the CPR transcontinental line in 1885 and the first to experience the demographic consequence of that resumption.

The short line built in 1906 between the CPR mainline and the Merritt coalfield was merely the first leg of what would eventually become the Kettle Valley Railway. The CPR started to lay track from Merritt along the Coldwater River in 1910, to connect the Nicola, Similkameen and Okanagan valleys. The first Kettle Valley Railway passenger train travelled from Penticton to Merritt in 1915. The Canadian Northern Railway completed Canada's second national rail line in the same year, and the Pacific Great Eastern connected tidewater and inland BC from 1916.

John Chelahitsa was a Syilx leader living in Douglas Lake country. John Tetlenitsa was a Nlaka'pamux chief living on a reserve across from the town of Spences Bridge, where James Teit lived. Teit, by birth a Shetlander, was their "hand."[20] Together they organized a gathering of Interior chiefs in Spences Bridge in the spring of 1910. There they prepared a statement of grievances and proposals for their redress, which they presented to Prime Minister Laurier that summer in Kamloops.

Their memorial is one of the most haunting texts the history of British Columbia has generated. It is firstly an Indigenous history, of the fur trade and the gold rush and subsequent settlement:

> *For a time we did not feel the stealing of our lands very heavily. As the country was sparsely settled we still had considerable liberty in the way of hunting, fishing, grazing. ...However, owing to increased settlement in late years, this has become changed, and we are being more and more restricted to our reservations which in most places are unfit or inadequate. ...Except we can get fair play we can see we will go to the wall, and most of us be reduced to beggary or to continuous wage slavery.*

It is secondly an Indigenous proposal for correction to and redress of their circumstances. It invites the Dominion government to work with the chiefs to provide their people with the same livelihood opportunities as settlers.

> *We have no grudge against the white race as a whole [or] against settlers...but we want to have an equal chance with them of*

> *making a living.....For the accomplishment of this end we and other Indian tribes...are now uniting and we ask the help of yourself and [your] government in this fight for our rights....We demand that our land question be settled and ask that treaties be made between the [Dominion] government and each of our tribes, in the same manner as [was] accomplished [by] the Indian tribes of other provinces of Canada, and in the neighbouring parts of the United States. We desire that every matter of importance to each tribe be a subject of treaty, so we may have a definite understanding with the government on all questions...between us and them.*[21]

The chiefs waited two years for an answer, and when it was delivered it was not what they wanted to hear. There would be no treaties. Instead, the provincial and Dominion governments agreed, there would be an investigation of the circumstances of the Indigenous peoples of BC. Indigenous title would not be investigated. The dismissal of title-and-rights negotiations that occurred then confronts all of us in British Columbia today as land-and-rights negotiations and judicial opinions begin to right old wrongs.

To sum up, the Nicola Valley at the start of the Great War was a metaphorical rural property, with two houses on it. The bigger, newer house had been recently enlarged. Its inaugural agrarian purpose was its first floor, and its industrial purpose a second-floor addition. The smaller, older house on the property was both haunted and occupied by the successors of the people who were once sole occupants of the property and by the ghosts of their ancestors.

Of the nine men pictured in "Delegation of Native Chiefs from Western Canada…May 1916," three were Nicola Valley residents. John Chelahitsa, a Syilx leader (*front row, second from left*), lived near Douglas Lake. John Tetlenitsa, a Nlaka'pamux leader, lived across from Spences Bridge, and is in the back row, second from the left. James Teit, standing beside him, resided in Spences Bridge. The men went to Ottawa to meet politicians.

Canadian Museum of History 36002.

In the pages that follow, ordinary men are remembered—as soldiers, mostly, but also as men with birthplaces, usually distant, and competencies, mostly now lost. Some of their survivors are remembered, too: a father who championed the welfare of veterans; the children who never forgot their uncle; a widowed mother who raised a family alone; and another who remarried to help her raise her family. In the pages that follow, all are remembered firstly as individuals and secondly as the collective creators of legacies that both help and hurt us today—*that we might live.*[22]

The *Merritt Herald,* the *Ormsby Review* and *British Columbia History* have published versions of some chapters of this book.

Michael Sasges
Merritt and Vancouver
2014–2018

The First Three:
"It Sure Was Something Hellish"

The first three men from the Nicola Valley to die in the First World War were a carpenter, a collier and a drifter before they volunteered. They were Britons by birth. They had soldiered before. And they were all members of the same unit, the 5th Canadian Infantry Battalion (Western Cavalry), when they died.

Robert Davidson, the coal miner, died first, on April 25, 1915, in Belgian Flanders. John Enoch Birch, the carpenter, and John Clyde McGee, he of no trade or profession save soldiering, were the next to die, on May 24, in French Flanders.[23]

Rapid and unprecedented assemblies and passages of men and materiel preceded their deaths. They endured and inflicted shot and shell of unprecedented lethality.[24] They also endured a weapon of unprecedented horror, one new to all the Western Front armies except the Germans.

The first valley volunteers for military service left Merritt 11 days after the United Kingdom declared war on Germany. (That declaration committed the Dominions like Canada and the Imperial possessions like India to war.) They began to leave British Columbia 23 days after the declaration. They left Canada for the United Kingdom barely two months after the declaration. And they left the UK for France barely five months after that.

The officers of the local militia regiment, the 31st BC Horse, put volunteers on trains on August 15, 18 and 19, 1914. Great Britain had declared war on August 4. "Pathetic scenes at local depot" accompanied the departure of the August 15 volunteers, the August 21 *Merritt Herald and Nicola Valley Advocate* reported. The men were only going as far as Kamloops. There they joined other British Columbia volunteers awaiting railway passage to the Valcartier training camp, outside Quebec City. They started to leave Kamloops on August 27, on one of 100 trains commissioned by the Dominion government to move volunteers to Valcartier.[25]

The largest military convoy yet to cross the Atlantic took the volunteers from Canada to the British Isles for further training. A squadron of Royal Navy warships led more than 30 transports carrying almost 31,000 men and 7,600 horses. When the last transport steamed out of the anchorage at Gaspé Harbour, 21 miles separated it from the first to leave.[26] (Physicians had found all the soldiers aboard medically fit after examination. All had been inoculated, and all had been issued uniforms and equipment. All had attested that they would follow their orders dutifully and would serve for the duration of the war. The attestation papers inform much of *Once Well Beloved*.)

Davidson died in a defensive battle during which the Anglo-French armies denied their German foes a town and the countryside in its vicinity. The battle is known as Second Ypres. (First Ypres occurred in the fall of 1914. Third Ypres, also known as the Battle of Passchendaele, occurred in the summer and fall of 1917.) Ypres was an ancient textile-trade town in Belgian Flanders. The Germans wanted it, and their Anglo-French adversaries wanted to keep it.

The Germans wanted Ypres so badly that they launched their April 22 attack with poison gas, inaugurating the use of that weapon on the Western Front. (They first used it three months earlier against Russia.) "That first devastating chlorine-gas attack...launched a chemical arms race [on the Western Front], as well as a parallel race to protect soldiers against asphyxiation, damaged lungs, blindness and burns," writes First World War historian Mélanie Morin-Pelletier, who organized an exhibition on the weapon for the Canadian War Museum, Ottawa.[27] Davidson, Birch and McGee were probably all gassed on April 24, the day before Davidson died. "All ranks suffering from sore eyes and choking coughs," the keeper of the 5th Battalion's war diary wrote.[28]

April 25, the day of Davidson's death, was a brutally long and trying day for his battalion. From 4:00 a.m. Germans maintained a "very heavy artillery bombardment" on the battalion's trenches. From 7:00 a.m. German soldiers in houses behind the battalion began to sweep it with "very obnoxious" machine-gun fire. At about 10:00 a.m. soldiers from a British

regiment "streamed past, having thrown their rifles away."
At about 1:00 p.m. the general officer commanding the 2nd
Canadian Infantry Brigade ordered the 5th and the adjacent
8th battalions to retreat. (That officer was Arthur Currie of
Victoria, who would eventually command all Canadians in
the field.) At around 4:00 a.m. on April 26, 24 hours after the
start of German shelling, the 5th Battalion's colonel thought
the retreat complete, his men "dead beat, gassed, starved, and
short of water."[29] More than 100 5th Battalion soldiers were
dead, wounded or missing. The battalion had left Canada for
England with 44 officers and 1,094 men.[30]

Birch and McGee died in the battle of Festubert, an
offensive battle in which Allied soldiers tried to force their
German foes to give up countryside. Their battalion launched
its attack from an orchard. The battalion war diary reports
the men "went to bed with darkness" on May 23, were roused
at 11:30 p.m. and began at midnight to take up their attack
positions. They took their objective, a German machine gun
redoubt called K5, and occupied it until midnight of May 25,
when another battalion relieved them.

McGee's circumstances-of-death card says no more than
"Killed in Action." Robert Davidson's card is equally spare.
Birch's card is detailed: "During a charge made by his Battalion
on the enemy lines at Festubert and just after he had gained
a footing in the German trench, this soldier was shot through
the head and instantly killed." (The Canadian military began
to issue helmets to its soldiers in 1916.[31]) The casualty count
from 5th Battalion's May 24 and 25 was at least 150 killed,
wounded or missing.

The three soldiers were Britons by birth. Davidson and McGee were "Clyde Waters" Scots, the former born in Ayrshire and the latter in Renfrewshire. Birch was an Englishman, from Manchester. (Of the first contingent soldiers, 70 per cent were born in the British Isles.) Davidson and McGee had both served in a British Army Highland regiment, the Argyll and Sutherland Highlanders, Davidson for 10 years and McGee for 7. Birch had served in a Royal Engineers volunteer, or territorial, battalion, in Lancashire. McGee was 30 years old at his death, Birch was 33, and Davidson, 41. (The average age of a Canadian Expeditionary Force soldier was 26.) Birch and McGee were bachelors. Davidson was married and the father of two boys. (About 20 per cent of CEF soldiers were married with children.)

Davidson and his wife, Isabella, had emigrated in 1909, crossing from Glasgow to Montreal. Neither then nor in 1911, when they were enumerated in Ladysmith on Vancouver Island, were they parents. When Robert volunteered, however, they were the parents of two boys. Isabella, four-year-old Robert, and two-year-old David left the Nicola Valley within months of Robert's death to live with Isabella's mother in Scotland. "A very large gathering was at the station to wish [Isabella] 'bon voyage,'" the August 13 *Merritt Herald and Nicola Valley Advocate* reported. Friends and neighbours had raised money to help her on her way, and she wrote the first of the many letters from widows and parents the newspaper would publish before the war's end, expressing her gratitude for the kindness of her neighbours. John Birch's mother in Manchester, too, received assistance from valley residents. Friends of the dead soldier

Vernon. 1914.   31st. B.C.H.   423.

One of the first men to share his battle experiences with Nicola Valley newspaper readers was cattleman H. H. Matthews, above. This photograph shows Matthews at the then-new Vernon military camp in the spring of 1914, barely a year before Second Ypres, and the first exposure of Canadian soldiers to Great War battle. After the war Matthews made the military his life. He died a general officer in Ottawa.

City of Vancouver Archives AM54-S4-: Mil P290.07.

organized a lottery that raised "about forty dollars," his tool chest the prize.

The first deaths point to some characteristic features of the Nicola Valley First World War experience.

First, at least at war's beginning, a number of Nicola Valley men had soldiered before or were training to soldier, or to soldier again. The local militia regiment, the 31st BC Horse, never fought a battle—at Valcartier the Canadian Expeditionary Force authorities broke up the country's mounted militias—but it was a remarkable military organization nonetheless. Two of the regiment's founding officers were eventually general officers. Charles Leonard Flick (1870–1949) was the first and only 31st BC Horse officer commanding. In the valley he was a merchant, newspaper editor and justice of the peace. In the Great War he was a regimental and brigade commander and eventually a general officer in Mesopotamia. H. H. Matthews (1877–1940) was the Canadian Army's adjutant general at his death. In the valley he was a cattleman, polo player, hospital director and fundraiser, and Church of England warden.

Second, anyone who wanted to know about battlefield conditions could know—or could know eventually. Throughout the war, the valley's newspapers published letters from soldiers overseas, sent to friends in the valley or directly to the newspapers. British and French military authorities did not encourage the owners and editors of newspapers to assign war correspondents. The publication of letters from the front written by soldiers from the valley made up for the lack of news from journalists and military representatives.[32]

The first letter published by the *Herald* after Second Ypres appeared in the June 4 issue. It was a private letter from 22-year-old Malcolm McAuley, a letter from an ordinary man about extraordinary experiences. "Dear Curley . . . I got a bullet right through the face." He also reported the use of gas. "When the Germans sent over the gas fumes it sure was something hellish. I did not get much of the gas, but I saw lots of them that did and any one who gets a good dose dies in agony, and any one who gets a small dose lives in agony. I have seen it both ways and I know." The second letter home was published in the June 11 *Herald.* Its author was H. H. Matthews. "My regiment . . . was the only one of the allied forces in the trenches that did not give way when gassed by the Germans."

The first letters after Festubert were published in the *Merritt Herald and Nicola Valley Advocate* and *Nicola Valley News.* Both were private letters. The author of the *Herald* letter was a 5th Battalion soldier, Bill Murray. "We had a bayonet charge on the morning of the 24th of May and we lost quite a number of the boys again. Jack Birch of Merritt and Corp. McGee of Princeton were killed. . . . We took the trench and got them on the run, we certainly rubbed it into them." The author of the *News* letter was an unidentified Lord Strathcona's Horse trooper who saw men from the valley carrying another, wounded, to the rear. "I gave him my water battle, and I guess he will be OK." The wounded soldier, Cecil Scrim, had been a lumber salesman before he volunteered. The military returned him to Canada in October 1915 after three months in hospital and another one and a half months in a convalescent camp in

England. A medical board had ruled him medically unfit for further service.

Canadian military authorities could and did censor letters home, but the continuing publication of letters from valley soldiers through war's end suggests they couldn't censor everything. The circumstances of the authors of the June letters may account for the "full and frank" quality of the letters. Three of them were in hospital when they wrote. Their letters were unlikely to be intercepted and read by the officers assigned to censor correspondence. The fourth author was a member of one battalion writing about another. His officer possibly saw nothing of consequence to censor.

A third characteristic of the first three deaths is that casualties were both high and disproportionate to the gains and losses. Second Ypres "cost . . . nearly 500 men killed, wounded and missing for us alone," Matthews said in his letter. When the 8th Battalion (Winnipeg Rifles) left Canada for England in October 1914, it left with 47 officers and 1,106 men of other ranks. The 8th and 5th Battalion casualties exemplify the Canadian War Museum's assessment of "Second Ypres": "The Canadian Division's trial-by-fire at Ypres earned the Canadians a reputation as tough and dependable troops, but they had paid a high price: some 6,000 casualties over the [first days of the] battle."

Lastly, the Canadian experience with the first gas attack on the Western Front meant all the battles the Canadians fought and all the firing lines and trenches they occupied were fought and occupied in the presence of the gas weapon, whether used or not. This was not true for the British, French and German armies who fought the first nine months of the Great War without resort to the gas weapon. Only the Americans, who came into the war two years after the first use of gas, fought all their battles in the presence of the gas weapon.

In circulating the news of the first deaths, the *Merritt Herald and Nicola Valley Advocate* did not acknowledge their significance. They were the first of the Great War, and the first since the Boer War. The headline atop its May 14 front-page notice of Robert Davidson's death is underwhelming and inaccurate: "Merritt officer killed in action." Davidson may have been a temporary non-commissioned officer, as a result of his previous service, but he was not an officer. "Father of two first from valley to die in war" might have approached the historic moment. The family circumstances were reported in the story, but the first-casualty circumstances were not.

One further letter reflects the strength of the connection between the first volunteers and the Nicola Valley. Published in the September 10, 1915, *Herald,* its author was a soldier from the valley who had gone overseas after the first contingent soldiers and had met survivors of Second Ypres and Festubert. "Merritt ought to be mighty proud of the first boys that left there for the front, and all I can say is that they are mighty lucky to be alive."

The body of John Enoch Birch was never recovered. He is remembered on the Canadian National Vimy Memorial, among more than 11,000 Canadian soldiers presumed to have died during the First World War in France. The body of Robert Davidson was never recovered either. He is remembered on the Menin Gate Memorial, with "55,000 men who were lost without trace during the defence of the Ypres Salient in the First World War."[33] John Clyde McGee is buried in the Le Touret Military Cemetery in France. There, almost 1,000 British, Dominion, and Imperial soldiers are buried.[34]

• •

NEXT: A cowboy who died in 1916 is remembered by family in the Nicola Valley to this day. The cenotaph in Merritt, however, remembers Thomas Charters under another name.

"Tommy" Charters:
"Nothing Special to Report"

Thomas Charters is the Nicola Valley's best and worst remembered Great War sacrifice. Family living in the valley today remember him. The cenotaph in Merritt, however, does not.

On the cenotaph, Thomas Charters is T. Tilamoose. No man with this surname, or anything like it, served as a Canadian soldier in the Great War. In the Charters family, he is "Uncle Tommy," says Mary Charters, a director of the Nicola Valley Museum and the widow of one of Thomas's nephews, the late William Charters. "We've always known that Tommy signed up and everything," Mary told the *Merritt Herald and Nicola Valley Advocate* in 2016, when it published my Thomas Charters discoveries in its Remembrance Day issue. "We have a postcard that he sent back from when he was in England."

He was Thomas Charters when he volunteered, when he wrote his will, and when he died, on October 12, 1916, at the Somme.[35] He was Thomas Charters when the October 27 *Herald* reported his death. ("The Casualty lists this week contain the names of three Nicola valley men, one of whom has died of wounds.... Pte. Thos. Charters of Aspen Grove...made the supreme sacrifice.") He is Tom Charters on the "roll of honour" that hangs in St. Michael's Anglican Church in Merritt, and he is Thomas Charters in the First World War Book of Remembrance in the Peace Tower in Ottawa.

Almost a century later, there is no explanation for the "T. Tilamoose" inscription on the cenotaph. Perhaps Thomas Charters was too well remembered. His death likely spared him a court martial; a few returning soldiers might not have wanted his name to appear. More likely, he was too poorly remembered.

Thomas Charters was an Indigenous cowboy. He grew up in the high country, and he lived and worked there and elsewhere before he volunteered. He was also a Catholic. In the recently industrialized, Protestant valley bottom, he was an outsider.

There was no champion to take up his cause. His parents were dead. His mother's second husband had troubles of his own. His official next of kin had quit the valley, although his half-brothers were there for the 1921 census of Canada. (Perhaps they requested the *nom de guerre*; perhaps they were never consulted.) Further, there was no chief or missionary or Indian Agent to advocate for him. Thomas Charters never lived on a reserve, where his memory might have been kept

Tommy Charters had this studio portrait done in Spokane, Washington, in 1912.

Courtesy of Mary Charters.

alive, and he was not a member of any parish. The churches he might have attended had no resident priests to notice his absence or pursue his remembrance.

Thomas Charters's mother, Pauline Sisyesq'et, was a Secwépemc woman from Thompson country. His father, George Tinamelst, was a Syilx man from Douglas Lake country. (This surname may be the source of the Tilamoose inscription.) Pauline's marriage to Harry Charters in 1899 is the only surviving evidence that Thomas's birth father had died some time before: the wedding could not have proceeded if Rev. J. M. LeJeune, OMI, was not convinced Pauline was a widow. The reading of the banns, and the profession of some of the most memorable words in the English language, preceded the wedding: "If any of you know cause, or just impediment, why these two persons should not be joined together in holy matrimony, you are to declare it."

The death of Thomas's father was not registered with provincial authorities. His mother's death was not registered either, but it was recorded in a front-page story the *Herald* published on December 15, 1911, under the headline "Pauline the Good gone over divide." The "kindness and hospitality" she extended "many a freighter and traveller" while in her father's home was one reason for the obituary's prominent display. "She felt no hardship in getting up from her bed in the middle of the night and cooking a meal for a weary traveller who was hungry and cold and had luckily hit her cabin." Her first marriage was of interest. She and her first husband, "a full blooded Indian," did not want to "live on the reservation" and "bought 160 acres near Aspen Grove, and there they lived for several years."[36] Her second marriage also generated acknowledgment: Harry Charters was the son of one of those 40 men named in that first enumeration of Nicola Valley voters from 1875. (His mother was one of the Indigenous women not mentioned in the near-contemporaneous local directory.) The *Herald* story said Pauline died of pneumonia and was buried on the Shulus reserve, below Merritt.

Pauline was the mother of at least seven children. She had three children by George Tinamelst—Thomas, Saul and Lily (or Lilly)—and four by Harry Charters—William, Robert, Sarah and Josephine (or Jose). In the 1891 census of Canada, Pauline and George were together with Thomas and Saul. Thomas was four years old. In the 1901 census, Harry and Pauline were together with Thomas, Lily, William and Robert. Thomas was 13, the enumerator recorded, and had passed 10 of the previous 12 months in school. In the 1911 census Harry and Pauline were together with Thomas, Lily, William, Robert and Josephine. In the 1901 census Thomas and Lily were described as Harry's son and daughter. In the 1911 census they were described as Harry's stepson and stepdaughter.

The Indigeneity of the households was and was not recorded by the enumerators. The 1891 enumeration records that Pauline, her husband and their children were "Ind." That description was no more than the enumerator's opinion. The 1891 census did not record race or cultural affiliation; the enumerator's observation was probably made as a result of a request from the Department of Indian Affairs. The 1901 census included questions about both colour and origin: all the members of the household were described as "R," for "red," with the blunt racism of the day, and "English." The 1911 census asked only the racial origin question, and in that year all the members of the household with the exception of Pauline were recorded as English. Either the 1911 enumerator misrepresented the race of members of the household or he misunderstood the instructions.

The *Merritt Herald and Nicola Valley Advocate* was certain that Thomas Charters was no Englishman. Later that same year he was one of seven "Indians" fined for drunken behaviour in Merritt over the Dominion Day weekend. Thomas paid the $5 fine. Harry Charters, Pauline's widower, was a "half breed" in a *Nicola Valley News* story about his prosecution in February 1916 for drunken behaviour. Harry too paid his $5 fine.

A second significant characteristic of Pauline's households that set them apart from others in the Nicola Valley was their Catholicism. Pauline, her husbands and their children were recorded as Roman Catholics in the three censuses. Harry Charters had converted, probably to marry Pauline—his parents were both Anglicans, according to the 1881 census. His baptism and his marriage to Pauline occurred on the same day in 1899, at the mission church on the Coldwater reserve.

The Missionary Oblates of Mary Immaculate had maintained missions among the Syilx and Secwépemc peoples since the 1860s, and they built churches in the valley, all located on Indigenous reserves, but they did not maintain a resident priest to minister to the needs of the faithful, Indigenous or settler, in the Nicola Valley. The Roman Catholic archdiocese of Vancouver consecrated the first church in the valley not located on a reserve, Merritt's Sacred Heart, in 1911.

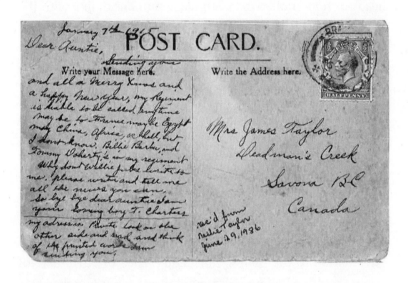

Thomas Charters was in a training camp in England in 1916 when he sent this postcard to his mother's sister.

Courtesy of Mary Charters.

The religious attestations of the people of British Columbia were totalled and published. In 1911 almost 60 per cent of people enumerated in BC professed an affiliation with the Church of England, the Church of Scotland or the Methodists, and barely 15 per cent with the Roman Catholic Church. In the Yale and Cariboo enumeration district, the percentages were 55 and 25. In Pauline's subdistrict, the Nicola, 10 of the 40 heads of household were Catholic, a number in line with the Yale and Cariboo as a whole.

Thomas Charters volunteered for overseas service in Vernon, in October 1915, just about where and when a cowboy from the high country might be expected to make a consequential turn in his life. His work year was over, and Vernon, with its military encampment, was easily approached from the upper Nicola along the Salmon River trail. He might even have made the trip to Vernon on a rancher's dime, driving cattle down the Salmon River to winter pasture in the north Okanagan, or to market.

When he volunteered, he also volunteered some personal information to the military, including place of birth, date of birth, "trade or calling," and marital status. In October 1915 Thomas Charters was single, and he was a cowboy. He was born on November 16, 1890, in Aspen Grove. He signed his name with the diminutive "Tommy." His birth year was probably not 1890. His year of birth in the 1891 and 1901 censuses was given as 1887, and in the 1911 census as 1888. And he was probably not born in Aspen Grove, but in the vicinity of the Nicola-Similkameen wagon road. The 1901 census and his mother's second wedding certificate locate the family home at Courtney Lake, on the trail—north of Aspen Grove by about five miles. Rev. LeJeune recorded Courtney Lake as the location of Pauline's "residence when married."

Pauline and Harry Charters were residents of Courtney Lake when the 1901 census-taker visited their home. They lived on 320 acres, and there were two houses and five outbuildings on the property. The occupied house had three rooms, the enumerator recorded. At an altitude of about 1,033 metres, Courtney Lake is about 425 metres above the forks of the Nicola and Coldwater rivers, where the town of Merritt lies. It is also about 13 miles, or 21 kilometres, south and east of the forks. Pauline's home would have been a welcome landmark for Indigenous freighters who controlled the transportation of goods between the Nicola and Similkameen valleys before the Kettle Valley Railway took that business away. Ranchers and their cowboys drove their stock through and around the lake twice a year, to and from their leases south and west of the wagon road. It was on that wagon road that Harry Charters, in March 1912, declined a drink of whiskey offered by a drunken man travelling to Aspen Grove from Merritt. The man was later found unconscious, and within hours he had died in the hospital in Merritt—of exposure, in the opinion of the attending physician.

When Tommy volunteered, he named his 13-year-old half-sister, Josephine, his next of kin. In the event of his death or injury, she could be contacted through the Aspen Grove post office. (He also later willed his back pay and personal effects to her.) Some time later, Josephine Charters left the valley. The medal card in Thomas's service file says she was in Savona, in the Thompson, at least for a while. (She was probably staying with family. Her mother was born on the Deadman Creek reserve, across the Thompson River from Savona.)

Thomas was eligible for the British War Medal and the Victory Medal. As her half-brother's next of kin, Josephine was to receive his campaign medals and a memorial plaque and scroll acknowledging his death in service. Notations on the medal card suggest the military sent the medals, but not the plaque and scroll, to Josephine at Savona. "M[edal] & D[ecoration]. Miss Josephine Charters, (Half Sister), Savona, BC P[laque] & S[croll]. Unable to locate next of kin." She had probably changed her name after the military dispatched the medals but before they were ready to send out the "P & S." She married a rancher by the name of Archie Davies, in Princeton, in the Similkameen countryside, on November 2, 1920. (Catholic bride and Methodist groom found a neutral cleric, a Presbyterian minister, to solemnize their marriage.)

Barely a year passed between Tommy's enlistment and his death. He and his battalion, the 54th Battalion (Kootenay), arrived in England on December 2, 1915, and in France or Belgium from August 12, 1916. He passed 47 of his English days "confined to barracks." He was punished for drunkenness twice, for "conduct prejudicial to good order and military discipline" once, and for an overnight absence. He was fined $2 and $6 for the drinking and $1.10, a day's pay for a private soldier, for the overnight absence. He passed 10 of his days in France enduring field punishment for being "whilst on Active Service Drunk." The number of his last field punishment is unreadable in his service file. If it was Field Punishment No. 1 he might have been fettered and cuffed, secured to a fixed object, a fence post or wagon wheel, for example, for two hours daily, and worked, when released from stationary confinement, "as if he were under a sentence of imprisonment with hard labour," in the words of a military law manual prepared for Canadian officers. If it was Field Punishment No. 2, he was spared the stationary confinement.

In both England and France, Tommy was prosecuted and punished "summarily," that is to say, by the officer commanding the battalion rather than by a court martial. In England the 54th Battalion's colonel, A. H. G. Kemball, remanded only one man to a court martial, for the uniquely military infraction of leaving a post without orders. In France in September 1916, Lt.-Col. Kemball sent five men to courts martial. Three of them were sergeants accused of drunkenness. "Sentence of court martial held on 3 sergeants on 7th promulgated. All were reduced to the ranks," the battalion's war diary noted on September 15. Thomas Charters, if his first field punishment didn't persuade him to keep out of trouble, was destined for a court martial—if not on the next transgression, then certainly on a subsequent offence. Courts martial could impose sentences that were harsher than any sentence an officer commanding could impose.

Thomas Charters was sentenced to his 10 days of field punishment on September 19. He died of wounds on October 12. "Nothing special to report," the war diary reported of that day's events. "Casualties 3 OR [Other Ranks] wounded." Thomas Charters did not die in battle, but he did die on the battlefield.

His battalion first saw action later that month, in the assault of a German defensive position called Regina Trench.

Thomas Charters's circumstances as Indigenous soldier and his experiences with civilian and military penalties for drinking deserve comment.

First, the contribution of alcohol to the dissolution of Indigenous cultures and the debilitation and death of Indigenous people is a much-recorded and much-examined Canadian shame. *Looking Forward, Looking Back*, one of the final reports from the Royal Commission on Aboriginal Peoples (1991–1996), is an important chronicle both of government efforts to prohibit alcohol possession and consumption by Indigenous people and of the effects of alcohol on the population.

An early record of the effects of alcohol on the Indigenous peoples of the Nicola Valley is dated 1878. In that year, Chief John Chelahitsa's father proposed to surrender to the Dominion government a Nicola Lake fishing station that had been allotted to his people 10 years earlier. He complained that settlers in the vicinity were debauching his people with whisky. The Dominion government declined.[37] Thirty years later, the start of rail service between the "forks" of the Nicola and Coldwater rivers and Spences Bridge either increased the circulation of alcohol in the lower valley or the surveillance of Indigenous alcohol use—or both. Six months before Thomas Charters's arrest in Merritt, Indian agent E. B. Drummond prosecuted two suppliers of liquor to the Indigenous residents of the lower Nicola Valley. He publicized both his presence in the valley and its cause: "Mr. Drummond's visit in the valley is to investigate the traffic in whiskey which is being carried on between the depraved white man and the Indian. We trust that his mission will be rewarded, and that the guilty parties will receive the maximum penalties of the law," the December 16, 1910, *Nicola Valley News* commented. Drummond sentenced one supplier to four months in the provincial jail in Kamloops, and the second to three months.

Of Indigenous soldiers in the Great War, *Looking Forward, Looking Back* estimates "well over 3,500 status Indians" volunteered for military service. "Many more tried to enlist and were rejected because of poor health or limited education. ... Their contribution was well received, and most Aboriginal people found acceptance as partners in the country's war effort." The report estimates the "status Indian" death toll at more than 300. The Nicola Valley's most distinguished soldier, then and now, was a cowboy from the upper valley, George McLean, of mixed Indigenous and settler descent. His "conspicuous gallantry" at Vimy Ridge in 1917 earned him a Distinguished Conduct Medal. Only a Victoria Cross was considered a greater honour. The valley also figured prominently in opposition to the conscription of Indigenous men. James Teit, on behalf of the Allied Indian Tribes, of which John Tetlenitsa was a director, co-authored at least one denunciation of the Dominion government's conscription intentions. Cabinet exempted Indigenous men from conscription in January 1918.

Thomas Charters's occupation before he volunteered illuminates a characteristic of life in the Nicola Valley in the first two decades of the previous century. The horse was an essential component of valley life. Many of his fellow soldiers earned their living behind or atop a horse before the Great War and soldiered with horses during the war. Charters could probably ride faster and further that any of them. He was also a horse breaker, a cowboy who trained horses to take a saddle or a harness, and, further, a rodeo competitor, Mary Charters says.

The relationship of Indigenous communities to the horse provides one of the most spectacular images, mind's eye only, of nineteenth century British Columbia. Yearly the Indigenous peoples of the Interior gathered at Chapperon Lake in Douglas Lake country for an early-spring fishery. "They have a race course, and for so many horses, and for their encampment and fishing purposes and feed for animals, require a considerable space," wrote the reserve commissioner in 1878, explaining his decision to create a fishing reserve on the lake.[38] Almost 40 years later, a horse sold by John Chelahitsa to the British Army was "the finest specimen of a horse bought in the interior," in the opinion of the officer who bought it.[39] The Great War was a good war for the owners of Interior horses generally. The British Army dispatched its first horse-buyer to the Nicola Valley in September 1914.

Douglas Lake Ranch provided each of its cowboys with half a dozen horses, none of them younger than four years old.[40] Valley ranchers used draft horses in their hayfields. Colliers worked around "pit ponies" from boyhood. (The Nicola Valley Coal and Coke colliery stabled its draft animals above ground.) As indispensable as the horse was in those decades in the valley, its necessity was coming to an end. As the October 3, 1913, *Merritt Herald and Nicola Valley Advocate* reported: "Mr. F. B. Ward, manager of the Douglas Lake Cattle Co., has purchased a Ford car.... Mr. W. Capp of the Nicola Valley Garage made the delivery and spent a few days at Douglas Lake giving Mr. Ward instructions as to handling."

Thomas Charters is buried with more than 1,300 Great War soldiers, a few of them German, in the Warloy-Baillon Communal Cemetery Extension in France. Since the publication of the 2016 *Merritt Herald* story on Thomas and the identification of his place of burial, a grandson of Mary Charters's late husband has provided the family with a picture of the grave marker.

. . . .

NEXT: A grieving father and a widowed mother transform their individual pain into community gain.

Vimy: "May God's Richest Blessing Rest upon You All"

Canadians, controvertibly, waited until 1917 to close out the nineteenth century and start on the twentieth. In that year the Canadian Corps captured three heights of land in France and Belgium: Vimy Ridge in the spring, Hill 70 in the summer and Passchendaele Ridge in the fall. At Vimy and Passchendaele, the corps seized countryside the Germans had denied other Allied armies. At Vimy, the four Canadian divisions in Europe fought together for the first time.

The feat of arms at Vimy Ridge was of little consequence to Allied victory over the Germans in 1918. It eliminated German observation of some French countryside, and it initiated Allied observation of the same. But it was of great consequence to Canadians, immediately and eventually, at home and on the battlefield.

The success of the inaugural Canadian Corps operation, in the opinion of the Vimy Foundation, "symbolically showed the strength of Canadians when they fought as one. It was also important that the Canadian Corps, [a] small colonial unit, had managed to do what both its former colonial powers [France and Great Britain] could not do in retaking the ridge."[41]

Vimy emboldened the Dominion government to challenge British assumptions about Canada's attachment to the United Kingdom—not to the country itself, but to its ambitions in peace and war. As the *The Canadian Encyclopedia* puts it, "Vimy soon became emblematic of Canada's overall experience in the First World War—especially its 60,000 war dead—a sacrifice that convinced Prime Minister Robert Borden to step out of Britain's shadow and push for separate representation for Canada and the other Dominions at the Paris peace talks after the war. This was followed in later decades by Canada's increasing push for autonomy from Britain on the world's stage—a desire triggered, in part, by Canadian sacrifices in the war."[42]

There is irony in treating Vimy as a starting line from which Canadian leaders began to imagine and project Canadian interests independent of British, or Imperial, interests. British infantry, British engineers and gunners, and British military planners and administrators assisted at Vimy. A British general officer, Julian Byng, commanded. Upon his elevation to the English peerage, in 1919, he took the title of Byng of Vimy.[43] Lord Byng Secondary School, on Vancouver's west side, is one British Columbia memorial to the general.[44]

The memorial cross on the ridge. "Ersatz Crater" was in front of the position from which the 72nd Battalion attacked on April 9, Seaforth archivist James Calhoun reports.

Seaforth Highlanders of Canada.

There were and are doubters about Vimy's significance. The Canadian who replaced Byng as commander of the Canadian Corps, Arthur Currie, thought Vimy was not the corps's most consequential effort. In his opinion, the successes the corps achieved in the last months of the war were more consequential. (Two of the last three deaths of men from the valley occurred in those months.) In the years leading up to the battle's centenary, historians have considered not only the battle itself, but the history of its significance to the nation.[45]

Four of the men named on the Merritt cenotaph died at Vimy: two as the Canadian Corps prepared for the assault, one on the day of the assault and one as the Canadians defended the gains the assault had achieved. Three of these men were colliers born in England and Scotland. The fourth was an old soldier and railwayman born in Norway.

The first of the four to die was the youngest. David Hogg was 23 when, as a member of the 47th (British Columbia) Canadian Infantry Battalion, he died in a trench raid on March 31. The officers organizing the assault on Vimy Ridge were determined to discover what and who was in front of the Canadians and how the Germans might defend themselves during a major assault. There was a cost to the knowledge gained, a blood price, and David Hogg paid it.

The raiders passed almost 30 minutes in no man's land and German trenches before withdrawing, one of the officers who led the reconnaissance recorded in the battalion's war diary. No man's land was so "ploughed up and soddened by rain" that some of the soldiers lost all sense of direction. The trenches the raiders reached were either flooded or "badly crumped," or destroyed, by artillery explosions.[46] The Germans had not completely abandoned them, however. The raiders brought back two "11th Bavarians" after killing some of their comrades in an exchange of gunfire, and the shoulder straps of some "15th Bavarians" after killing them. They also tried to remove the corpses of two Germans killed by artillery fire, "but being wedged in by timbers we could not extricate them to secure identification."

The Germans were probably expecting the Canadian raid: "The enemy opened an intense barrage on our lines and on no man's land at ZERO minus 2 minutes." Subsequently "heavy fire from Artillery of all calibres" harassed the Canadians continuously. Of the 100 Canadian soldiers who participated in the raid, 58 were killed, wounded or missing.

The second to die was the oldest of the four, Ingebrigt Busk. He was one of the thousands of soldiers in railway and construction battalions who supplied ammunition, equipment and clothing, food and forage, and water to the tens of thousands of engineers, gunners and infantry, and their draft animals, assembled below Vimy Ridge. A member of the 1st Canadian Labour Battalion, Busk died on April 1, 55 miles from Vimy. As he returned to his billet in the vicinity of Abbeville, on the Somme River, he was hit by a train or locomotive.

"Men not fit for service in the trenches," in the words of Library and Archives Canada—meaning older and disabled men—served in the labour battalions. When Busk volunteered in 1916, he said he was 45. He was probably 55 or thereabouts. The 1910 United States census—the last census in which he appeared before volunteering—records his age as 50. At

For the centenary of the Battle of Vimy Ridge, the Seaforth Highlanders of Canada commissioned the restoration of the memorial cross erected on the ridge by members of the 72nd Battalion. Conservator Tara Fraser is cleaning the base, or plinth, of the memorial. John McInulty's name is in the first column, sixth from the bottom.

Fraser Spafford Ricci Art Archival Conservation, Surrey.

enlistment in the US Army in 1887, he said he was 25 years old. (The register of enlistments that records Busk's service gives no reason for his discharge in 1890, and notes his character was excellent.)

John McInulty died on April 9, the day of the assault on Vimy—the only one of the four to die in the actual attack. A native of Ayrshire, Scotland, he was a member of the 72nd Battalion (Seaforth Highlanders of Canada). McInulty was one of 85 Seaforths killed or presumed killed on April 9 and 10. Another 124 other members of the regiment were wounded. "The fighting was very heavy and we suffered many casualties," wrote Lt.-Col. J. A. Clark, a Vancouver lawyer, in a preliminary report on the fighting dated April 11.

The circumstances of McInulty's death are unknown. Did he die in the open or in the battalion's regimental aid post? Quickly or slowly? By shot or shell? There is no record; he was merely "killed in action" at the age of 34. Though the circumstances of John McInulty's last day cannot be known, his battalion's circumstances immediately before and after zero hour, 5:30 a.m., April 9, 1917, are well attested.

The battalion was by then a battered fighting force.[47] When the 72nd left Canada for the UK in April, 1916, it consisted of almost 1,100 soldiers and 34 officers. Lt.-Col. Clark led 400 soldiers into the battalion's assigned tunnel on the evening of April 8.[48] He sent about 300 of them out into no man's land on April 9. The battalion's objectives demanded that its soldiers cross ground visible from Hill 145 and Hill 120, the two highest German positions on the ridge. Hill 145 was not cleared until the afternoon of April 10; Hill 120, or "the Pimple," not until April 12.

David Hogg's uncle, Alexander Hogg, died on the Pimple on April 13. The day was a "splendid day—snow nearly all gone," the keeper of the battalion's war diary wrote. Alexander has no known grave; perhaps he was a victim of the diary's intermittent "shelling by enemies [correct] heavies." The battalion left the Pimple by day's end. "All companies relieved by 11:30 P.M." Alexander Hogg was 37.

The April 20 *Merritt Herald and Nicola Valley Advocate* recorded David's death; the April 27 *Herald*, Alexander's. The editor put both deaths on the newspaper's front page. The Methodist faithful in the valley held a memorial for uncle and nephew, as well as a third soldier, Jack Harrower, who had died in a French hospital, not wounded, but ill. "An exceptionally large crowd was in attendance." The newspaper did not record the deaths of Busk and McInulty immediately.

It recorded Ingebrigt Busk's death in its October 12, 1917, issue, in a story written by a *Herald* reporter who had interviewed Ingebrigt's son, Otto, himself a returned soldier. It might be said that Ingebrigt Busk died twice: ignobly, in France, and nobly, in the Nicola. Otto Busk thought his father died a member of a "working party subjected to a terrific bombardment from the Germans" in the vicinity of Vimy Ridge. The two colonels who reviewed the report of a military court of inquiry that followed on his death had another opinion. "He had no right to walk on the railway track which apparently he was doing when killed by a train," and "he was to blame" for his death. (The army probably never recorded Busk's death in the casualty lists it circulated among Canadian newspapers.)

The *Herald* did not record John McInulty's death until the first list of the valley's dead was circulated at war's end. He was probably barely known in the valley. One record of his link to the valley is no more than an intention: Merritt was his destination, he told the purser of the vessel that carried him to the New World from the Old in 1911. Another record of his presence in the valley is actually a record of his daughter's presence. When Harriet McInulty married in 1937 in Victoria, she said her place of birth was Merritt. Harriet and her sister, Mary, had each placed a floral tribute at a war memorial in 1921 on Vancouver Island. "The words were, 'In loving memory of our dead daddy, from your little girl,'" the May 28 *Cumberland Islander* reported. Inclusion of McInulty's name on the memorial outside the Cumberland Great War Veterans Association hall was contested, but the production of his local employment record by the organizers of the memorial and the presence of his daughters at the memorial unveiling answered all challenges.

The deaths created three widows: Bergithe Busk, Margaret Hogg and Mary McInulty. Bergithe Busk was living with her daughter in Spokane, Washington, when her husband died. Mary McInulty was in Vancouver. But Margaret Hogg was in the valley when her husband, Alexander, died. David Hogg's parents, Francis and Lois, were not, but they were in Vernon, not far away.

The two Hogg households had been in the Nicola Valley since 1910. In April of that year, Alexander and Francis, either half-brothers or cousins, crossed from Liverpool to Halifax. Francis's wife, Lois, and their children, including David, sailed

David Hogg had the top stoop to himself in this photograph of his family outside their Collettville residence in about 1911. Below their big brother are, from left to right, Hannah, Andrew and Eunice, with Lois and Frank in front.

Collection of Linda Buzzell.

with them. (Their destination was Middlesboro, they told the purser.) Alexander's wife, Margaret, and the couple's son, another David, crossed from Liverpool to Montreal in September 1910 with a stated destination of Merritt.[49]

In 1901, when the England and Wales census was conducted, Francis, Lois, Alexander and Margaret Hogg were all living in County Durham, England, in colliery villages on the River Tyne. Married since 1893, Francis and Lois were the parents of three children: David (born in 1894), Hannah (1896) and Eunice (1900). The birth in 1903 of Andrew completed the family. Alexander and Margaret, married in 1900, were the parents of another David (1901). They would have two more children in British Columbia: May in 1911 and Allan in 1915.

As emigrants, the two Hogg households had left a geography in which industrialized resource extraction—that is, resource extraction and carriage increased and accelerated through the use of steam power—was pioneered.[50] As immigrants, they arrived in a geography where the industrialization of extraction and carriage was just getting under way. They brought with them competencies that BC desperately required. The two Davids belonged to the fourth generation of Hogg men to work a coalface.[51] Their great-grandfather, Robert Hogg, was a coal miner no later than 1841, the year a British census first recorded occupations. Grandfather David was underground by 1871. Francis was underground by 1891; Alexander, by 1901.

The Hoggs also brought with them a wonderful history of accommodations with and resistance to the Industrial Revolution—a history of workplace and parliamentary agitation over worker safety and the distribution of the wealth generated by coal mining, of the pursuit of universal male suffrage, of production and consumer co-operation, and of Methodism and the English working class.[52]

The most important contribution of English Methodism to the material well-being of ordinary men and women was its inculcation of reading, writing, public speaking, listening and leadership skills among its faithful. Methodism was an evangelical denomination, its first mission to the English labouring class, and every Methodist was a candidate missioner.

Frank Hogg's life is a pronounced example of a Methodist sensibility informing and influencing an individual's activities and aspirations. The first record of Francis Hogg using his literacy and numeracy for the good of his community is an employment record. In the 1901 England and Wales census, he described himself as a checkweighman. Checkweighmen were selected by colliery employees, and paid by them, to confirm colliery management's measure of the coal the hewers produced. Theirs was a statutory position, imposed on employers by parliament. The last record of Frank Hogg putting his skills to use is also an employment record. The February 23, 1940, *Merritt Herald and Nicola Valley Advocate* story about his death five days earlier reported that he had been a bookkeeper for local "commercial houses" for many years.

In between are other occupational records that suggest Frank Hogg was determined not to pass all his years underground. In 1910, he was an insurance agent, he told the purser of the vessel carrying him to Canada. The English co-operative movement had been offering its members life insurance for 40 years by the time Frank emigrated. He may well have helped Tyneside collier families finance proper burials for their kin. In 1915 he quit underground work, probably forever, to undertake one of the most forlorn occupations in human history: he became an internment-camp guard, his prisoners German and Austro-Hungarian nationals.[53]

In his 30 years in the Nicola Valley, Frank Hogg's activities generated considerable journalism. He started a local chapter of a temperance-advocacy group, the International Order of Good Templars, soon after his arrival. He was secretary of the local co-op by 1913, when he gave a 15-minute talk on the co-operative movement. As secretary of the Collettville Improvement Association, he successfully petitioned Merritt city council to extend electrical service to Collettville in 1914. He was adept, clearly, at identifying, or imagining, the needs of the people around him, and at broadcasting what he knew.

His most important voluntary efforts in the five or so years between his arrival in the valley and his departure for guard duties was undertaken on behalf of Methodism, mediating the relationships of the older, agrarian Canadian Methodist families who started to arrive in the valley in the 1870s and the industrialized English Methodist families who started to arrive in the 1900s. The presence at Frank's funeral of an "insider" witness to his efforts among the Methodist faithful, old and new, suggests that his work was admired and remembered. A. R. Carrington, one of two ushers at the funeral, was secretary of the Nicola Valley Methodist Mission in the early twentieth century. A native of Victoria, Carrington came to

the valley with his parents in 1872 and was a farmer and merchant when Frank arrived in the valley.

The earliest notice of Frank's 30-year affiliation with first
the Methodist and eventually the United Church of Canada
was published in the *Herald*: he was listed as one of the enter-
tainers at the "first of a series of Pleasant Saturday Evenings in
the Methodist Church." He eventually served as a member of
the local Methodist Quarterly Official Board and a lay leader
of the local United Church.

Frank Hogg's most important voluntary association in the
last years of his life was with the Canadian Legion. He was the
secretary of the Legion's Nicola Valley branch from at least
1932. "His painstaking efforts for war veterans will long be
remembered," the *Herald* commented in its front-page story
about his death, funeral and burial. Legion members helped to
organize a funeral worthy of a member of consequence. A pipe
band accompanied the flag-draped coffin into the church, a
piper played a lament and a bugler played the Last Post at the
cemetery. Stores lowered their blinds as the funeral procession
passed. "The large congregation and turn-out of automobiles
in the funeral procession demonstrated the esteem and regard
which was held for the deceased in the community." Lois,
Frank's wife, had died six years before, but their surviving
children—Hannah, Eunice and Andrew—and their spouses
and children were present. Sister-in-law Margaret Hogg was
also there.

Remarkably, burial was one of the subjects in an address
Frank made to branch members two weeks before he died. The
Legion's Last Post fund had paid for the funerals and grave

markers of 13 Great War veterans buried in the local cemetery, he told the gathering. "We as a Legion Branch do not exclude those who were not affiliated with us at their decease," the notes he prepared for the meeting read. "They claim our comradeship."[54]

"I feel certain he died in the way that he would have desired—working for others," observed a Canadian Legion correspondent who had received, on the same day, a report from "Comrade Frank" about a Legion fundraiser in the Nicola Valley and the report of his death.[55]

Margaret Hogg's life is not the pronounced demonstration of Methodism at work that her brother-in-law's life was, but it is profoundly memorable. Her demonstration of fortitude and her consideration for the community on the occasion of her husband's death are admirable and enviable. The *Herald* published her words on May 4, 1917: "I desire to take this means of expressing to all our friends our heartfelt thanks for the many kind words of sympathy and comfort spoken to us since our great bereavement. ... *May God's richest blessing rest upon you all.*"

In considering a future without her husband and the father of her children, Margaret probably considered leaving the Nicola Valley. Isabella Davidson, widow of the first soldier from the valley to die in the Great War, was gone barely four months after her husband's death, home to her mother in Scotland. Bergithe Busk and Mary McInulty, the two other women made widows by Vimy, had already left when their husbands died. The *Herald* twice speculated that Margaret might leave in 1918, though she was not expected to go far.

This portrait of the Alexander and Margaret Hogg family was probably made in 1912, perhaps for the christening of the couple's second child, May. At the right is May's older brother David.

Collection of Linda Buzzell.

April 12: "Mrs. A. J. Hogg was a passenger to Vancouver Tuesday morning. ...Mrs. Hogg may decide to remove to the coast to reside permanently." May 24: "Mrs. A. J. Hogg and children left yesterday morning for Vancouver, where they expect to take up their residence." They didn't, and in July 1919, Margaret, May and Allan instead left Merritt, and David, for England. Twice burned, the newspaper reported that the purpose of the journey was to visit relatives. Members of the family, however, have long thought Margaret probably intended to remain in England. But in January 1920, Margaret, May and Allan returned. In October of that year, she received her Memorial (Silver) Cross, "the first memorial cross that has been received in Merritt," the October 8 *Herald* noted. And in November 1921, at the Merritt cenotaph dedication, "the largest outdoor gathering ever assembled in Merritt," Margaret Hogg presented a wreath.

There was probably little keeping Margaret in England in 1919, and more pulling her back to Canada. Her oldest son, David, was in the valley. Brother-in-law Francis and sister-in-law Lois were there, too. Francis and Lois had certainly put down roots. In 1921 their two daughters, Hannah and Eunice, were married women, both living in Collettville, just outside Merritt. Hannah Ovington was by then a mother of three. She had married a neighbourhood boy in 1913, like her the child of a collier from County Durham. He volunteered for service in the Great War but never made it to the front. Eunice Rowbottom had no children yet: she and her husband Edwin had been married for barely half a year when the census enumerator visited.

In the 1921 census, Margaret and her three children were all under one roof in Collettville. She owned the house, she told the enumerator. Her son "Davy" had earned $600 in the previous year as a coal miner; Margaret did not provide the enumerator with her own income. She had received a Canadian government pension since Alexander's death. Whatever her reasons, Margaret made a choice at the end of 1919, and she decided for Canada.

In the valley after the war, Margaret's two youngest both graduated high school, a notable educational achievement in the '20s and '30s in Canada, made all the more notable as the achievement of the children of a lone-parent household. After graduation, Allan pursued a career in communications, first as a telegraph operator for the CPR, second by pursuing a Dominion government wireless operator's certificate, and eventually in the Royal Canadian Air Force. May was a provincial civil servant for 10 years before she married. She, too, was an examination-taker. "Miss Margaret May Hogg, who is on the staff at the government office here, is listed among successful candidates at the provincial civil service examinations for stenographers," the July 10, 1931, *Herald* reported. David, the oldest, was a musician all his life and a sailor. During the Second World War, he joined the merchant navy, and he later worked as a steward on Alaskan cruise ships. He never married, and he always came back to Merritt when he wasn't at sea.

In 1936, Margaret Hogg was one of 6,200 veterans and their families and Memorial Cross mothers and widows present for the dedication of the Vimy Memorial in France. The Canadian

Legion organized the pilgrimage and subsidized individual expenses.[56] "One's head almost swims," Margaret Hogg told *Herald* readers of seeing the more than 11,000 names inscribed on the memorial, among them her husband's. In England, after the dedication, Margaret presented herself as a Canadian and was received as a Canadian. "To me was given the honour," she said, to lay a wreath at the cenotaph in London in a ceremony organized by the British Legion. Canadian veterans in their Vimy pilgrims' khaki berets, and their families and the Memorial Cross mothers and widows in their blue berets, marched to the cenotaph from a Westminster Hall reception, a distance of about 500 metres. While visiting her "ain folk" in the north, Margaret's beret again signalled her nationality. At a gathering in County Durham, as "the only Canadian with a beret," she was "often accosted with 'Hello Canadian,'" Margaret recalled.

Margaret Hogg was both a Memorial Cross wife and a Memorial Cross mother. Flying Officer Allan Hogg, RCAF, died January 28, 1943, in Prince Rupert, BC, when his patrol plane crashed in the harbour during landing. It is impossible to say how rare or unique her circumstances were: Veteran Affairs Canada has never counted the number of women who lost both a husband and a child in Canada's two world wars. "Allan never knew his father and Allan's child will never know him," Margaret told the *Herald*. That child, Linda Buzzell, is today a resident of Penticton.

Margaret Hogg died in 1958, in her 77th year. She had told her family she did not want to be buried in the valley: she wanted to be buried with her son, Allan, in Belleville, Ontario. Margaret's son David accordingly took her remains across the

"Jack" Nash: "Excellent Work Performed under Fire"

T he contribution of well-born Britons to the British Columbia settlement experience has engaged historians, popular and scholarly, for many years. Jean Barman estimated their numbers 35 years ago: perhaps 25,000 or so of the 175,000 Britons who immigrated to British Columbia between 1891 and 1921 were the adult children of the British middle class. She is also the author of the ultimate qualitative assessment of their role: "This generation of Britons exercised influence beyond their numbers."[57] By birth, education, denominational attachment, recreational pursuits and marriage, John Foster Paton Nash was one of those Britons.

"Jack" Nash was a brave soldier. His competency and composure during the battles that claimed the lives of John Enoch Birch and John Clyde McGee earned him a Distinguished

John Foster Paton Nash is the man on the left in this undated
photograph. The clergyman is James Thompson, who delivered
Nash's eulogies in 1916 and 1917. The women are "Miss McPhaile,"
behind Thompson, and "Mrs. Meikle."

Nicola Valley Museum and Archives PAS105.

Service Order. He was not the only officer from the Nicola Valley to receive a DSO, but he was the only officer from the valley to receive a DSO and die. The *London Gazette* reported his award, the official notice of Royal favour, on August 25, 1915: "For conspicuous gallantry through the action at Festubert 22–24 May. He repaired the telephone wires personally under very heavy fire. Capt. Nash was again brought to notice for excellent work performed under fire at Fleribaix and Gravelstafen." Nash was the 5th Canadian Infantry Battalion's signals officer.

John Foster Paton Nash survived a year of the Great War. He died on April 23, 1916, two days after his 50th birthday. It was Easter Sunday. The 5th Battalion's circumstances that day were desperate. According to the war diary, Nash died seven days after his battalion entered the trenches and one day before it left them. The day of his death was the third of four days of heavy German bombardment, the intensity of shot and shell forcing battalion headquarters to find another position. He may have died in the presence of a visiting general officer. Louis Lipsett, the officer commanding the 2nd Canadian Infantry Brigade, "was badly shelled where Capt. Nash was killed," the brigade's war diary reported.[58]

John Foster Paton Nash had lived in the Nicola Valley from at least 1886. On November 11 of that year, he pre-empted land—that is, purchased unsurveyed acreage from the province—in the upper valley. The location of the land on the register that records the transaction is not particularly helpful: it merely says "Lot 772." But the inclusion of names like Nash's Field and Nash Creek on modern maps locates the

pre-emption. The latter "flows SW into Salmon River, NE of
Salmon Lake," according to the provincial government's BC
Geographic Names website. In buying Lot 772, with its creek
running through it, 21-year-old John Foster Paton Nash had
put an ocean and most of a continent between himself and
family tragedy.[59]

Born in 1866, in a London suburb, Nash passed his boyhood in the care of his father's relatives. His mother, Amelia
Jane, died in 1868, probably in childbirth. His father, Thomas,
subsequently suffered a mental breakdown, and was a resident
of a private asylum from at least 1871. In that year's England
and Wales census the enumerator recorded father Thomas
suffering from "melancholia." The 1871 census also finds the
couple's oldest child, 11-year-old Edith, residing with one of
Thomas's sisters and her husband, eight-year-old Stewart
at boarding school, and seven-year-old James, five-year-
old John, and three-year-old Amy living with another of
Thomas's sisters.

There was money. The family, including father Thomas
until 1863, owned trading companies in the United Kingdom
and Brazil. All three sons boarded at King William's College,
Isle of Man; middle son James took two degrees at Oxford;
and John attended a merchant marine college. None of the
children inherited. When father Thomas died in 1885, he left
his estate of more than £70,000 at probate to a brother. In
leaving his estate to one beneficiary, Thomas Nash authored
a bequest typical of a man of his means and time and place.
In leaving his estate to a man who was not his eldest son,
however, he was doing something unusual. The terms of

Thomas's retirement from the trading companies in 1863 may have dictated the bequest.[60]

A merchant marine cadet in England in the 1881 England and Wales census, John Foster Paton Nash was a Nicola Valley "farm labourer" in the 1891 Canadian census. He does not make an appearance in the 1901 Canada census: he was probably in England, on his way back from South Africa and Boer War service with Strathcona's Horse. (When he volunteered in 1900, he reported his occupation as "cow-puncher.") He was discharged on March 16, 1901, in England, as a private soldier.

He had returned to the Nicola Valley by the end of 1901. On December 2 of that year he asked the military authorities in Ottawa to send his Queen's South Africa Medal clasps to Quilchena, Nicola Lake, "my address."[61] Two days before Christmas he put an $80 deposit down on 160 acres of Crown land along Quilchena Creek. He completed the transaction in February 1902, when he also applied for another 160 acres on Quilchena Creek, due him as a Boer War veteran. He received that land in November of the same year. The lot numbers suggest the properties were not contiguous. The 1911 census finds John Foster Paton Nash, rancher and fire warden, residing with a lodger in Quilchena, in the 16th of the 21 households enumerated in the subdistrict.

The local press first took notice of Nash in 1905. This first acknowledgement was no more than a record of his visit to the Similkameen, the first of many such reports of his travels in and out of the valley. In 1906 and 1907 he played polo, and the papers carried sporting news: "Guichon and Nash were conspicuous by their hard hitting" said the *Nicola Herald* on

September 6, 1907. Nash's teammate was probably the younger Joseph Guichon, not the elder. The latter was in his 57th year by the date of that polo match; the former, in his 28th. Nash and the younger Guichon also coordinated a Christmas week turkey shoot in 1907. "There was a fairly large attendance and some very close shooting for the birds," according to the *Nicola Herald* for December 27. In socializing with a Guichon, Nash had established a connection with a family that pioneered ranching in the Nicola Valley and BC.[62]

News that Jack Nash had entertained friends "at his far famed ranch, Fisherman's Rest" in February 1910 inaugurates the record of his activities that year. In March he announced that about 100 Nicola Valley residents had applied for membership in a shooting club he was organizing. "With thirty of more members obtained, the government will grant one rifle and 100 rounds of ammunition for every four members," the *Nicola Herald* account of his efforts noted. In March and April of 1910 Nash performed in two fundraisers organized by the Ladies Auxiliary of the St. John the Baptist parish in Nicola. He and Vicar Thompson arranged and performed a skit they called "Wanted, a Lady." (They were both single men, and they both came from Lancashire, Thompson by birth and Nash by childhood residency.) "The net proceeds will reach over seventy-five dollars." In May Jack's horse threw him "rather violently," and injuries to his back kept him in bed for more than a week. In June he received news that would determine the rest of his days: he had received a commission in the local militia regiment then being formed, the 31st Regiment, BC Horse. In July he received a Dominion government contract to supply telephone poles between Quilchena and Nicola, a distance of 9 or 10 miles. As a fire warden he would have known where the best standing timber was to be found.

His March announcement about the shooting club may have been a broadcast of his suitability for an appointment as game warden: the office of the game warden issued firearms licences. But he had a more significant advantage in his favour: game wardens were appointed by the attorney general, and Jack Nash was a local supporter of Premier Richard McBride's governing Conservative Party. He was elected "2nd Vice President" of the riding association in February 1911.

As a provincial fire warden and eventually a game warden, John Foster Paton Nash represented a central authority and its ambitions for the province's natural resources and their commercial exploitation. The BC Archives holds the record of the mounted patrols he completed as a deputy provincial game warden in the first three months of 1914. In those three months he passed his daylight hours either riding between settlements ("30th | Patrolled round Nicola to Merritt") or riding in the high country and backcountry. The purpose of his rides was to record the wildlife he and others spotted and to check firearms licences. He visited trapper camps, wood camps, railway-construction camps, cow camps, horse camps and Indigenous reserves. His diaries record these activities: "reported Indian to L. Guichon, JP ... Patrolled from Merrett to King's ranch on the Coldwater, visiting the Reservation on the way ... To the Douglas Lake Reserve and onto the Douglas Lake Ranch ... Always ride around [unreadable] the reserves when staying in Nicola." When in the backcountry and the high country, he inevitably ended his day at a ranch house: "Night at Lauder's ... night at Quinville's ... night at L.L.C.C. horse ranch." In January he passed 10 consecutive nights in the backcountry. "Snow is fairly deep in most places, and in drifts was up to the horse's stomach," he commented in the report on that month's patrols that he prepared for headquarters. "I saw several trappers, but no one seems to have had much success this year. I found several farmers without licences (Free Farmers' Licences), and am forwarding their names to Vancouver. They asked me for licences."

His work as a fire warden was also done on horseback. Unlike game warden work, however, fire warden work was seasonal, starting in the spring and ending in the fall. Guards passed the start of the fire season maintaining and adding trails and telephone lines. They passed the rest of the season supervising all permitted slash burns by loggers, farmers, and railway and road builders, and patrolling the province's forests by horse and boat. They were inevitably the first to hear about a wildfire or to see one. They were spotters first, and firefighters only secondarily. The forest branch annual report for 1914 noted that the early and correct responses by wardens were essential. "In a bad fire season ... poor judgment on the part of an inexperienced Guard may result in the unnecessary expenditure of thousands of dollars." The author of the report did not share any examples of poor judgment or unnecessary spending.[63] The same report described the 1914 fire season as "one of the worst in the history of the West." The Nicola Valley was not spared: "Fires raging on the surrounding hills: Much timber and property is being destroyed," reads a front-page

Note.—This Return must be carefully filled up, showing plainly how the time of Deputy Game Warden was employed, and forwarded to the Provincial Game Warden on the last day of each month.

DAILY DEPUTY GAME WARDEN'S REPORT

of Deputy Game Warden _J. F. P. Nash_ , Station _Nicola Lake_

District for the Month of _February_ , 1914

1st In the vicinity of Nicola Lake, up the Old road to Quilchena, and back. Camped at Nicola

2nd North of Nicola visited Mc Fosters wood camp, and one Trappers camp beyond back to Nicola.

3rd East and North of Nicola Lake visited Hoopers, Lamberts, Doings, settlers on Mountain, back to Nicola

4th Up New road to Mc Thompsons, and Bonds new settlers, back to Nicola.

5th To Winnie Ranch. on to Quilchena and back to Nicola.

6th To Quilchena stayed night — Reported to J. Guichon's Al Ranch.

7th Round Reserve, on to Cow Camp in field on Nicola River, on to Sanders Ranch stayed night.

8th Close about Sanders most of the day plenty of Prairie Chicken here

9th Visited Beadles and Miss Hawkings Ranchers, and country round night at Sanders.

10th Up to Hawking's property and back to Sanders,

In the first three months of 1914 John Foster Paton Nash patrolled the Nicola countryside as a deputy game warden. Pictured here is the first page of his February report to headquarters.

BC Archives, Provincial Game Warden records, Box 136, File 4, 1914.

headline in the *Merritt Herald and Nicola Valley Advocate* for August 14. ("Many enlist at first call of country: Local regiment expect[ed] to leave Sunday," reads another.)

The patrols by fire and game wardens were probably of greater consequence for the residents of rural Indigenous reserves than for settlers. Their foraging activities on their traditional territories were at stake. As the BC Archives introduction to the game warden files in its custody observes: "Conflicts between the provincial approach to the game resource and that taken by some Native Indians can be studied in this collection."[64] A statement from a man from Coldwater, made in 1913, a year before Nash's work as a warden began, is more memorable. To members of the Royal Commission on Indian Affairs for the Province of British Columbia he said:

> I want to explain to you how poor I am. You people know how poor I am—I cannot take a step anywhere, just as if I am standing on one leg right here today—Yes, I cannot take a step anywhere. If I am going to try to make a place outside where I am, the white people will pull me right back again.
>
> [Question]: How will the white people pull you right back again?
>
> Answer: Because they will not allow me to hunt or get my own food...even the Government are stopping me from hunting.[65]

Indigenous hunting, actual or imagined, certainly influenced the decision by the provincial government to station a deputy game warden in the Nicola Valley.[66] The provincial game warden file in which the eventual decision is discussed is a small file in the BC Archives, its contents a month's correspondence from May 1910. A letter from a Merritt resident to the attorney general opens the file with a complaint about out-of-season hunting of game birds and deer by Indigenous hunters. "As I am not an officer I do not wish to act. But hope your Department will take into consideration the advisability of appointing a proper person who will devote all his time ... [to] the protection of game." Later in the month, the letter's author attempted a private prosecution of an Indigenous man for hunting deer out of season. The case was dismissed. Both the letter writer and the justice of the peace who dismissed the prosecution wrote letters about the affair.

The JP wrote that extenuating circumstances prompted his decision. The accused pleaded guilty, but the chief of the Coldwater Band testified that a Department of Indian Affairs official had given him permission to extend to "poor Indians" the "privilege" of foraging as needed. "In consideration that they were under this impression, and it being a first case, I dismissed the case with costs, with the understanding that any further cases would receive the full penalty." He asked if the provincial game warden had any knowledge of this "privilege." The warden said he did not. "As the district is an Organized one Indians have no special privileges in the way of killing game of any kind, nor has [DIA] the right to give an Indian, or anyone else, authority to break the Provincial Laws," he wrote. He also gave the JP some sentencing direction: organize a game law prosecution to fit the accused's circumstances. For example, it might be preferable to convict on a charge of possessing venison out of season, for which the penalty was a fine ranging from $1 to $100, rather than a charge of killing a deer out of season, for which the minimum fine was $25. The attorney general asked the provincial game warden for his "views" on the dismissed prosecution and two pleas from the Merritt Athletic Club about the need for a game warden. The warden replied that he thought government would "have to do something for this district before very long." The Nicola Valley had a deputy game warden—not Jack Nash—from at least the fall of 1912. "The fact he did not receive his commission till the shooting season was open made the appointment look rather like locking the stable door after the horse was stolen," said the September 13 *Herald*.

John Foster Paton Nash did something exceptional on his way to war in the summer of 1914: he married. His bride, 29-year-old Eleanor Flora Wilson, had been in the valley since the spring. She was visiting one of her four sisters, Justina Geraldine, identified in the local newspapers as "Mrs. V. H. Harbord." The wedding occurred in Kamloops on August 17. It was a Church of England ceremony. Jack had probably left the Nicola Valley on August 15, on the first train that carried members of the 31st BC Horse and other volunteers north to Kamloops. There, the first BC volunteers for overseas military duty were assembling as they waited for the Dominion government to organize their transport out of province.

There are so many questions to ask about the wedding, but there is no way of answering them. There are no letters extant, no professions of love or of intent. The Isle of Man was one experience bride and groom had in common: both had passed some of their childhood there, he in the 1870s and she

14-09-142065   18065

VITAL STATISTICS ACT.

SCHEDULE F.—Marriage Certificate.

Marriage solemnized in the District of *Kamloops*

[stamp: GOVERNMENT AGENTS OFFICE / AUG 19 1914 / KAMLOOPS, B.C.]

No.	64
Name and surname of bridegroom.	John Foster Paton Nash
Age.	48
Condition, bachelor or widower.	W
Rank or profession.	Government Employee (Fire Warden)
Residence.	Nicola
Place of birth.	Surbiton, Lond
Name and surname of father.	Tom Nash
Name and surname of mother.	___ Stewart
Rank or profession of father.	Planter
Religious denomination of bridegroom.	Church of England
Name and surname of bride.	Eleanor Flora Wilson
Age.	29
Condition, spinster or widow.	S.
Rank or profession.	
Residence.	Nicola
Place of birth.	Pinxton, Derbyshire
Name and surname of father.	Henry Wilson
Name and surname of mother. (maiden)	Isabella MacArtie
Rank or profession of father.	Clergyman
Religious denomination of bride.	Church of England
Date of marriage.	August 19th 1914 (Aug 17. H.S.a)

Married at * S. Paul's Church, Kamloops, B.C., according to the rites and ceremonies of the Church of England, by † Licence

No. 47226

This marriage was solemnized between us { J. Nash
Eleanor Wilson

In the presence of { Lyonulf deMollemete
Lilian M. Rose.

(Signature of Minister or Clergyman) Henry S. Akehurst
Rector of Kamloops.

* Enter place and situation.
† Banns or license—give No. of licence.
20,000/3/1913.

On the Jack Nash and Eleanor Wilson marriage certificate, Nash reported that he was a widower. Neither a marriage nor a death that would have created that "condition" was recorded in British Columbia.

BC Archives Vital Statistics Agency marriage registrations, Reel B11384, Vols. 139-47, Registration record numbers 04713 to 050046.

in the 1890s. The Church of England was another. Jack was the grandson of a clergyman and the brother of another. Eleanor was a clergyman's daughter.

The 19-year difference in the ages of bride and groom is of more than prurient interest. Age disparity between spouses has long been a subject of study.[67] So have the circumstances of women like Eleanor Flora Wilson—originally, in the nineteenth century, as a problem in search of a solution. Eleanor was an unmarried woman in England, and ever since the 1851 England and Wales census revealed there were more women than men, and more female children than male children, such women were considered "superfluous." In the 1911 England and Wales census, there were 1.3 million more girls and women than men and boys among the 45 million inhabitants of England and Wales. In the last half of the nineteenth century, several organizations were created to make the problem go away by encouraging middle-class women to emigrate.[68] While there is nothing to indicate any emigrant organization helped Eleanor visit her sister, there is plenty to indicate that in marrying Nash, she was helping herself avoid a lifetime dependent on the succour of parents, siblings and their spouses, and, finally, on the children of siblings and their spouses. Neither of Nash's sisters appears to have married. Amy Nash was certainly a "spinster" in 1894 and 1929, the years in which she received small bequests.

There are British Columbia reasons to celebrate the marriage of Jack and Eleanor. She found an eligible bachelor, a relatively easy adventure in BC before the Great War, and he found an available "spinster," a much more difficult endeavour.

Single women were relatively few and single men relatively plentiful in BC when Eleanor and Jack wed. The 1911 census of Canada enumerated 160,000 single men and around 71,500 single women in British Columbia. They married in the first of two years in which the number of BC marriages declined, according to the *Canada Year Book* for 1916/17. In the last three years before the start of the war, about 4,900 marriages occurred annually in the province. The 1914 number is almost 4,300; the 1915 number, just under 4,000. The economy of British Columbia was retreating in 1914 and '15, and economic retreat is traditionally followed by a retreat in marriages.[69]

Jack and the Dominion government certainly provided for Eleanor. He assigned half his $2.60 daily pay to Eleanor, beginning in October 1914. (He fought as a captain, but was paid as a lieutenant.) The Dominion government granted her a wife's separation allowance while Jack lived and a widow's pension after he died. She was his sole beneficiary in the will he wrote in February 1915 as his battalion crossed the Channel from England to France. A notation on the copy of the will in his service folder is poignantly anticipatory of Eleanor's eventual circumstances: "Copied from Pay-book, Page 14. Original left in Pay-book, and returned to Mrs. J.F.P. Nash, 2 Church Park, Whitchurch Tavistock, S. Devon." That was still her address when she died in 1959, after an eminently Victorian widowhood of more than 40 years, surviving her widowed mother, who died in 1936, and a widowed sister, who died in 1956.

Eleanor and Jack Nash passed most of their brief married life apart: He was either in battle in Belgium or France, or training for battle in Canada, the United Kingdom or France. They may have had a few days together in Kamloops, as his duties permitted. (The train that took the first BC volunteers to the Valcartier training camp in Quebec departed Kamloops on August 27, 10 days after the wedding.) They may have kept each other's company before his battalion left the United Kingdom for the continent. (The first contingent of the Canadian Expeditionary Force arrived in the UK in October 1914; Eleanor returned to England later that month.[70]) They had three more opportunities to keep each other's company after his battalion left for the continent. He was granted leave, duration not recorded, in September 1915; a leave of eight days in November and December of 1915; and another in February 1916. Canadian officers serving in Belgium and France routinely passed their leaves in the British Isles. On the first anniversary of their wedding, he was in Flanders, in the trenches in the vicinity of Ypres, and she was in the United Kingdom, in Whitchurch. (They were probably together a month later.) There was no second anniversary. At most, Eleanor and Jack may have spent two months together during their married life.

The *Nicola Valley News* reported Nash's death on April 28, 1916. (The *Merritt Herald and Nicola Valley Advocate* probably also carried the news that day, but no known archival copy exists.) " 'Jack' was everybody's Jack," the *News* commented. "Happy go lucky, typical of the Englishman living the free life of the Westerner." His death generated two gatherings of Nicola Valley residents: one soon after the news arrived and one in February 1917. The small church of St. John the Baptist in Nicola was the scene for both. Vicar James Thompson was honouring both a friend and a St. John parishioner. Before the war, Jack Nash was a St. John "sideman," an assistant to the parish's churchwardens.[71]

"Representatives of nearly all the ranches in the district" attended the first memorial, the May 5 *News* reported. "From Douglas Lake to Merritt men and women from every denomination" attended the second. The *Herald* considered the gathering unprecedented, rightly or wrongly: "Never in the history of the valley has such a congregation assembled." At this second gathering, a commemorative tablet in Jack Nash's memory was unveiled. "The church was full and extra seating ... had to be requisitioned."

Returned soldiers provided an honour guard. "Many noticed with a thrill of exquisite pity that some of the boys ... were still suffering from the trying times they had been through." They might have been wounded or underweight. They might have been sick with one of the communicable diseases that bred and spread in the trenches, like tuberculosis, or hobbled by trench foot caused by too many days and nights standing in the cold, filthy water that flooded the trenches. They might have been gripped by a look, unfocused and vacant, called since the Second World War the thousand-yard stare. One of them unveiled the tablet. Rev. Thompson "preached a splendid sermon." The women of the parish "provided refreshments."

John Foster Paton Nash is one of almost 2,500 soldiers buried in Railway Dugouts Burial Ground, in Belgium. Outside the Nicola Valley, he is remembered on a memorial on the campus of King William's College, Isle of Man, and on a cenotaph in the churchyard at Whitchurch, Devon.

· ·

NEXT: As the Allied armies pushed the German armies out of Belgium and France, a new belligerent, the Spanish flu, launched a killing campaign around the world.

The Last Three:
"Died This A.M. 5 O'Clock"

O f the last three men from the Nicola Valley to die in the Great War, two were killed as the Allied armies drove the German armies out of Belgium and France in 1918. The third died in 1919, four months after Germany's political and military leaders sought, and received, an armistice.

The first of the last was John Paul, who died on September 29, 1918, in France. Norman Fletcher Lindsay died on October 31, also in France, of wounds suffered on October 9. The last of them was Fred King, who died on March 7, 1919, in England.

John Paul was a member of the 11th Battalion, Canadian Railway Troops. He was killed by a single enemy shell that landed on the entrance to a "sap," or trench, near the light rail line his battalion and others had been working on. A collier from Scotland, John Paul left a wife, Marion, and six children in the Nicola Valley when he volunteered in March 1916 for a labour battalion assignment. When he died, the *Merritt Herald and Nicola Valley Advocate* reported that three of his children were staying with a friend of the family in the valley; the other three were with Marion and her sister in Maine. Marion re-married in Merritt less than a year after John Paul's death. Her second husband was also called John, was also a miner and was also a native of Scotland. At the time of the 1921 census of Canada, John and Marion Clark lived on Clapperton Avenue in Merritt, with 10 children—four of them his and six of them hers—and a lodger. John Clark was a widower.

There is a certain poignance when a young soldier survives all his regiments' battles but the last. Norman Lindsay went to war in 1914 a member of the 5th Battalion and died in 1918, at the age of 25, as a member of the Fort Garry Horse. In between he was a member of a machine-gun brigade. He was there when Robert Davidson died during Second Ypres. He was there when John Birch and John McGee died at Festubert—indeed, he was wounded there. (He wrote a letter to the *Herald* to say he was recovering nicely.) He left the battalion long before Jack Nash's death. He joined his machine-gun unit in August 1915 and was a member of the Fort Garry Horse from January 1916. He was wounded again in 1918 and awarded a Military Medal that year, although no record explains why.[72]

Norman Lindsay was in the Nicola Valley because he wanted to be around horses, and eventually to ranch.[73] He passed his last night in the company of horses: "Died of Wounds/Was wounded by a high explosive shell in the back, while in charge of lead horses 100 yards North of Reumont, on

Members of the Fort Garry Horse, troopers and mounts, pass through a French village in December, 1917. Photographer unknown.

Library and Archives Canada MIKAN 3405682.

October 9th 1918," his circumstances-of-death card reads. "He was evacuated to No. 3 Stationary Hospital, Rouen, where he died sometime later." The shell killed three soldiers and wounded eight, as well as killing eight horses, the regiment's war diary reports.

Earlier on October 9, Fort Garry troopers had charged their German opponents on three occasions. One squadron killed "a great number of the enemy with the sword" and captured 200 prisoners, an after-battle report says. One squadron captured more than 40 German soldiers and six machine guns "before they could reach them with the sword." And one squadron achieved whatever it was ordered to achieve without mention of whether or not it used the sword.[74]

Norman Lindsay was an unusual young man for his time and place. He was born in Vancouver, he said when he volunteered in 1914, although a family history on the internet says he was born on Vancouver Island. The 1901 census locates his parents, Percival and Charlotte, his eight siblings and their one servant in Chilliwack, in the Fraser Valley. Percival was a farmer, he told the enumerator. The 1911 census locates the family on Vancouver Island.

Lindsay was a bank clerk when he volunteered, and as a member of a Bank of Montreal team he participated in a hockey game that provides an enchanting vision of the Nicola Valley before the Great War. Between his team and the Bank of Toronto team, 21 goals were scored. "Excitement reached fever heat time and again, as each goal was in danger, the ladies assembled being almost delirious," the *Herald* reported on March 27, 1914. Lindsay was a bachelor in 1914 and '18, his

Trooper Norman Fletcher Lindsay died after being wounded by German shell fire and "while in charge of lead horses," in the words of the Fort Garry Horse's war diary.

Lindsay-Vaughan-Irving Family Tree, ancestry.ca.

parents residents of a Beach Avenue apartment in Vancouver
when he volunteered and when he died. His father was a
lumber broker. Norman Fletcher Lindsay's death was never recorded by the *Herald*, by 1918 the only newspaper in the valley.

The last Nicola Valley man to die soldiering, Fred King, did
not die in battle or on the battlefield, but from complications
of the Spanish flu—or, as a note in his service file written by a
military physician records, of "purulent bronchitis & [bronchi-
al] area collapse & pneumonia." (There was an autopsy.)

The Spanish influenza pandemic contributed to the deaths
of perhaps 50,000 Canadians in 1918 and '19. That number,
added to the 60,000 Canadians who died fighting, means at
least 110,000 Canadians died prematurely between 1915 and
1919. The consequences of the pandemic were profound. "The
epidemic brought not only death but social and economic
disruption. . . . Children were left parentless and many families
found themselves without their chief wage earner. Armies on
both sides of the war were temporarily debilitated. Businesses
lost profits because of lack of demand for their products or
because they were unable—as a result of a reduced work
force—to meet the demand."[75]

The pandemic contributed to the deaths of about 800
Canadians in uniform. Fred King's Canadian Forestry Corps
recorded its first death attributable to the flu in September 1918.
"10 Lieut. Ball admitted to No. 20 Hospital with pleurisy and
influenza," the headquarters war diary reports. "16 . . . Advice
received from No. 20 Hospital Lieut. Ball dangerously ill,
pneumonia. 17 Lieut S.H. Ball died on No. 20 hospital." An
executive with a Montreal sawmilling and manufacturing

company before he volunteered, Sidney Ball was in his 40th year, a husband and father, when he died. The forestry corps's French headquarters were located in one of the places where the first outbreaks of the Spanish flu occurred: Étaples, on France's Pas-de-Calais coast.[76] There the British Expeditionary Force maintained a military camp of camps, in which as many as 100,000 soldiers from all over the Empire were billeted on any given day, training or recovering from wounds or illness, or awaiting assignment or reassignment.

A teamster from Aspen Grove, Fred King was in France from January 1917 until January 1919, mostly with the Canadian Forestry Corps and mostly in Normandy. In April 1918, he was sent to hospital in Rouen, the ancient duchy's principal city. There he was diagnosed with "myalgia" and sent to a convalescent camp. Muscle pain, even debilitating muscle pain, would have been an occupational hazard for the corps's loggers, sawyers, road-builders and teamsters. But it can also be a symptom of influenza.

On release from convalescent camp at the end of May 1918, King was in Étaples for a week before rejoining his forestry company. He took two weeks' leave in England in July and August. On October 5 he was transferred to the 29th Canadian Infantry Battalion, Vancouver's "Tobin's Tigers." (Forestry corps companies had been training for battle since April.) King's stay at the front was brief: he was in hospital in France from October 17, and in England from January 10, 1919, until his death on March 7. "4.3.19 Period of great respiratory distress early evening. . . . 7.3.19 . . . gradually becoming weaker. Died this a.m. 5 o'clock."

In the Nicola Valley that went to war in 1914 horses were
everywhere, working for and with people. Images of operations
in France by members of the Canadian Railway Troops, left, and
the Canadian Forestry Corps, right, demonstrate the continuity
of the relationship.

L'Exploitation par les Canadiens

The railway troop teams are grading the route of a light railway.
The forestry corps animals were log haulers. Fred King soldiered
with the forestry corps; John Paul, with the railway troops.

Library and Archives Canada MIKAN 3405529 and MIKAN 3523256.

Fred King is an intriguing man, but an unknowable one. Neither his life in the Nicola Valley nor his death in England generated any newspaper comment. The genealogical databases do not return any information about a man by that name with the birthplace and birth year that King gave when he volunteered in August 1916. (From the attestation paper in his service folder: "In what Town, Township or Parish, and in what Country were you born? San Francisco Cal. U.S.A. . . . What is the date of your birth? November 14th 1886.") "Fred King" was probably a *nom de guerre*. He was probably Italian, either born in Italy or born in the United States to Italian immigrants. The address of his next-of-kin was an Italian address. Sister Delfina King, or Delfina Burbone, was a resident of Tuscany. (He didn't put Delfina in his will. Inexplicably, perhaps mischievously, he left his estate to an Anglican church in Montreal, St. James the Apostle. How much, really, would a teamster possess to leave a church? He was also Roman Catholic, he said on his attestation paper.) And, whether a mistake of the writer of the notation or not, the "medical history sheet" in his service folder reports he was born in Italy.

The Spanish flu invaded the Nicola Valley quickly and lethally. The October 11, 1918, *Merritt Herald and Nicola Valley Advocate* announces the pandemic's arrival. The so-called "Spanish flu" was causing "havoc" across Canada, although not in the valley. It advised readers to avoid infected people and go to bed if they were infected. Two weeks later the *Herald* recorded the first death of local significance attributable to the flu. The man was not a resident of the valley, but members of his family were. The 34-year-old cattle broker, "in the best of health and spirits" before he died in Kamloops, was a typical case. The young and the old were not this pandemic's preferred victims. The same front page also recorded the decision of city council to close all schools, churches, clubrooms, theatres and pool halls in Merritt and ban all public assemblies in the city.

The November 8 *Herald* reported the first deaths of settlers in the valley: a husband and wife, parents of two children. The November 15 newspaper recorded four more deaths, one of them of a returned soldier; the November 22 paper, another three deaths. The November 29 *Herald* recorded no deaths, and the cheering news that city council had lifted the church closures so that "thanksgiving services" could be held. The Dominion government had asked that no services be held in November, to prevent the spread of the flu. The number of settler deaths reported to and recorded by the provincial Registrar of Births, Deaths and Marriages in November and December was seven; the number of deaths recorded in the *Herald*, nine.

The pandemic's passage through the Nicola Valley was devastating for residents of the valley's reserves. ("It is pointed out," wrote the *Herald* on November 1, "that not since the days of the smallpox has an epidemic carried off the Indians of British Columbia as Spanish 'flu' is doing today.") There are at least three death counts: 62, on four reserves, in November and December, reported to and recorded by the provincial Registrar of Births, Deaths and Marriages; 83 recorded by the BC Provincial Police constable in the valley; and almost 100 recorded in the service journal of the All Saints' Shulus mission church. Of a population of 600 or 700, as many as

one in six Indigenous people in the valley died of flu complications. From the service book: "About this date [the]
'Spanish Influenza' epidemic broke out on this reserve and
other reserves in the Nicola Valley. Services were discontin-
ued—the church as well as the school [and the] hospital being
used for housing patients. Nearly one hundred Indians died
in the valley." October 27 was the last Sunday in 1918 in which
Eucharist was celebrated at All Saints. (One parishioner took
communion.) It was not celebrated again until January 1, 1919,
and that service was in the mission house, not the church.[77]

Constable Percy Badman of the provincial police started
his involvement in the care of the Indigenous sick and dying
on October 28. On receiving a telegram advising him that a
number of Shackan Reserve residents were dead, he drove out
to the reserve. "Found on arrival situation was very serious,
Spanish Flu raging." On the next day Badman returned to the
reserve with food "purchased on instructions from the Indian
Dept." On October 30 he and the local DIA physician took
over the Shulus hospital, school and churches as "hospitals
to receive Indian sick suffering from Spanish Flu." On the
same day, he led a convoy of five cars to Shackan and other
Indigenous settlements below Merritt and "removed [the]
sick to Shulus." He also stopped people on their way to Shulus
for a potlatch from entering the reserve and asked the CPR to
stop them "from leaving this reserve as 90% were sick." On
October 31 he again directed removal of the sick and dying
to Shulus from other reserves. "Notified Indian Chief and
Captains that Indians from Lytton, Ashcroft, Lillooet Reserves
who were attending Potlatch on his Reserve must not leave

until given permission." On November 1 and 2 he removed the Indigenous sick from reserves he had not visited on previous days. On November 3 he "took sick with Spanish flu etc." He did not return to duty until December 10.[78]

The care of the Indigenous sick and dying at Shulus was a brave endeavour. At least two settlers died as a result of their work helping the sick at Shulus. Their names are Edith Menzies and John Forhnwieser. Edith Menzies and her parents had recently moved to the valley from the Lower Mainland in the hope that dry-clime residency would be better for her health. (She twice quit nursing school because of ill health before her parents organized the move to the Nicola Valley, her *Herald* obituary reported.) In the November 1 newspaper, she and another nurse were caring for about 50 people in Shulus; on November 8, she was under the care of physicians; by November 15, she was dead. She died on November 9, in the ranch house in which her parents were staying, and was buried the next day, the newspaper reported. She was 26 years old. Forhnwieser died November 12 in the "isolation hospital" provincial and municipal authorities had set up in Merritt city hall. There was a hospital in Merritt by 1918, but the authorities decided not to place settler residents ill with influenza there. "The general hospital is being reserved for all patients suffering from other ailments," the November 8 *Herald* reported. "There are ten patients in the general hospital, two of which are maternity cases. Two births have been recorded there during the past week." John Forhnwieser was Austrian by birth, an origin that barred him from Canadian Expeditionary Force service. "When the influenza epidemic broke out in this valley and the health authorities opened Shulus hospital for the treatment of the Indians, John Forhnwieser was one of the first to volunteer his services in any capacity." He, too, was in his 26th year when he died.

The Indigenous sick and dying resented their isolation, a November 8 *Herald* story on the Shulus ill suggests. The story reported them to be difficult patients. "The authorities and those in charge at the hospital find it quite a difficult task to keep the Indian patients quiet. They do not take kindly to the white man's method of treatment." In fact there was no treatment for influenza, beyond bed rest. There were, however, numerous Indigenous treatments for the respiratory ailments influenza introduced into a person, like pneumonia, the sickness that was often the cause of death. More than four dozen plant medicines, decoctions and infusions for the treatment of respiratory ailments, including pneumonia, were known to the Nlaka'pamux. Some of those "difficult" patients might well have had the knowledge and ability to treat themselves and others—their "being difficult" an expression of their frustration that their abilities and knowledge, or their requests for traditional treatment, were being ignored.

Additionally, the absence of Indigenous caregivers may have worsened the circumstances of Shulus patients, a possibility about which Indigenous leaders had cautioned. A confidential report from the commission on Indian affairs commented favourably on requests members heard that Indigenous women be trained in hospitals as nurses. Once trained they would serve in their home reserves. "Such services would be more acceptable to the Indians than if rendered by others and would go far to furnish what is now lacking and is almost impossible to properly provide for in the medical treatment and care of the sick on Reserves."[79]

The record of the pandemic's passage through Canada and the Nicola Valley is the record of a cruel and capricious (biological) tyrant inflicting new sufferings on a people already worn down by war. It is difficult, a hundred years on, to appreciate or comprehend so much coincidental misery. But in the work of Edith Menzies and John Forhnwieser we see the capacity of humankind to challenge terrible circumstances, and in the remarriage of railway-soldier John Paul's widow and her creation of a blended household of 10 children we find another.

John Paul is buried in the Duisans British Cemetery, France, among almost 3,300 other soldiers, including some Germans. Norman Lindsay is buried in the St. Sever Cemetery Extension, France. Almost 8,700 soldiers are buried there. Fred King is buried in the Basingstoke (Worting Road) Cemetery, in the United Kingdom.

Conclusion

For me, a native Vancouverite, the monuments to the British Columbia of the first two decades of the previous century have long been Victory Square and two office buildings nearby. My maternal grandfather was a Princess Patricia's Canadian Light Infantry soldier during and after the Great War. My mother and my siblings and I always visited Victory Square on "Armistice Day," as Remembrance Day was called in the years between Canada's two world wars. My wife, Marise, was another annual Victory Square visitor, to watch her mother's father and his old comrades parade. Across the street from Victory Square is the Dominion Building; down the street, the World Building, also known as the Sun Tower. The first, at 13 floors, was the tallest commercial building in the British Empire until the second, at 17 floors, was built. The first opened in 1910; the second, two years later. The cenotaph was unveiled in 1924.

The Nicola Valley has added other markers of my attachment to those decades of war and peace, industrialization and
fitful urbanization and factional government. These include
the three Protestant churches in Merritt, the extant railway
hotels (the Coldwater and the Adelphi), and the abandoned
rail beds and railway bridges that run along and across the
Coldwater and Nicola rivers. The concrete piers of the bridge
that once crossed the Coldwater to connect John Hendry's
colliery and Merritt and Thomas Shaughnessy's railway
are my Ozymandian ruins. Marise and I usually attend the
Remembrance Day ceremonies at the Merritt cenotaph;
friends and neighbours are organizers and participants or
parents and grandparents of participants.

To elevate 12 of the 44 men remembered on that cenotaph
into representatives of their time and place demands more than
assertion. It asks for demonstration. Here that demonstration
starts with an assertion about the province's natural geography. Settlement by Old World peoples occurred relatively
late, because the Canadian Cordillera was not easily reached
from the North Atlantic. It was not easily traversed, either,
because of its mountainous terrain. And it was only intermit-
tently cultivated, because arable land is sparse. Farmsteading
migrants were not, accordingly, the principal beneficiaries of
the settlement of the Canadian Cordillera.[80]

The absence of that agricultural energy or impulse turned
upside-down a 200–year pattern of settlement in North
America, east to west, Atlantic seaboard to the Rockies. But
grassland, minerals and timber were plentiful. Exploitation
of these natural resources was labour intensive, which made

industrial labourers the principal beneficiaries of coloniza-
tion. The 1,500 navvies Thomas Shaughnessy temporarily
employed to build the short line between the CPR mainline
and the Nicola Valley's coal measures were ideal colonizers.
The 400 miners employed at Nicola Valley collieries in 1912
were equally ideal. As Jean Barman writes: "Any search to
understand British Columbia's past is integrally linked to its
geography."[81]

Not one of the 12 well beloved was a farmer before he
volunteered. Not one was a farmer's son or a farm labourer.
In the Nicola Valley of the Great War, farmers were few, and
although ranchers were more numerous, they weren't many,
either. Some people in the valley, and their provincial government, wished it weren't so, but the countryside was too hot or
too cold, too high or too dry to support cultivation.

Eleven of the 12 well beloved were wage workers before
they volunteered. John Birch was a carpenter. Ingebrigt Busk
was a railway timekeeper before he came to the valley. Thomas
Charters was a cowboy. Fred King was a teamster. John Foster
Paton Nash seasonally policed the back country and the
reserves before he volunteered. Robert Davidson, Alexander
Hogg, David Hogg, John McInulty and John Paul were colliers. Bank clerk Norman Lindsay was a wage earner, too, but
probably presented as a salary man. John Clyde McGee, the
drifter, probably worked for wages when he had to.

Further, 10 of the 11 wage earners were employed, directly
or indirectly, in the industrialized extraction and carriage of
natural resources: Busk, Charters, King, Lindsay, Nash and
the five colliers. The occupations of the 12 well beloved are

one component of their nomination as representatives of their British Columbia. Their origins are another.

Men and women from the British Isles dominated the settlement of the Canadian Cordillera. Eight of the 12 well beloved were British born. Three of them were born in metropolitan geographies whose contributions to the colonial and commercial ascendancy of the British Isles, indeed to the ascendancy of the North Atlantic world, are inestimable: Birch in Manchester, McGee in Greenock (down the River Clyde from Glasgow) and Nash in suburban London. The other five Britons were natives of hinterland geographies, in the south of Scotland and the north of England, in which industrialized resource extraction and carriage was pioneered. Their birthplaces were new settlements, or settlements enlarged by railway extensions and expanding collieries, in countrysides where agriculture continued to sustain people. Fundamentally, the Nicola Valley of the early twentieth century was a British Columbia iteration of the industrialized hinterland of the north of England and the south of Scotland.

The contributions of Britons to the settlement of British Columbia has a couple of meanings. The "identification [with the UK] ... stood apart" from the rest of Canada, Jean Barman has observed. "British ways were not transplanted into British Columbia because they existed elsewhere in Canada. The link was with Britain itself."[82] That direct link was never more memorably professed than during the First World War. Ninety of every 1,000 BC residents volunteered. In the Prairies and Ontario, the proportion was 75 per 1,000; in the Maritimes, about 50. ("While British Columbia's uneven sex ratio played a role, so did the province's British character," Barman writes of the robust BC volunteer experience.) The link had tremendous, enduring reach in British Columbia during the twentieth century, certainly in electoral politics and in employment relations. All eight Britons among the well beloved had the vote. The achievement of universal male suffrage in the UK had occurred in their fathers' lifetimes. Statutory endorsement of trade unions, too, occurred within living memory. These were birthrights not diminished by a change of residency.

Geographer and historian Cole Harris has presented another aspect of the British settler experience in the province. The conversion of the Indigenous geographies of the Canadian Cordillera into the colonial geography it is today repeated a British experience of land dispossession, inhabitant immiseration and involuntary relocation. The infamous clearances in Scotland and enclosures in England, which prepared the British Isles for the world's first industrial revolution, destroyed lifeways that had secured ordinary people to the land since time out of mind. If enclosure and clearance were not part of the lived experience of people who came to BC from the Isles, the attitudes toward property inculcated by that experience probably were. Those attitudes energized settler occupancy of Indigenous territory, Harris observes. Settlers from the Isles assumed "most of the land they encountered...was waste, waiting to be put to productive use; or, where Native people were using the land, that their uses were inefficient and therefore should be replaced." They took, without treaties or compensation. And their governments denied any taking back through surveillance and criminalization of the residents of the reserves and through their refusal to acknowledge Indigenous title.[83]

By occupation, by origin and by privileged status, as beneficiaries of government measures that favoured their residency over Indigenous residency, the Nicola Valley's 12 well beloved are representative of the British Columbia of the first two decades of the twentieth century. As such they are also representatives of an inimitable historic experience, made inimitable by the province's physical and cultural geographies.

+ + +

Restoration of an old house in the Merritt neighbourhood of Collettville introduced me to the people of the historic Nicola Valley. Research in the provincial archives in Victoria and in municipal and church archives in Vancouver and at the Nicola Valley Museum and Archives in Merritt turned them into treasured company. I did the archival reading in pursuit of a Simon Fraser University graduate degree. I defended, and SFU published, *Colliers and Cowboys: Imagining the Industrialization of British Columbia's Nicola Valley*, in 2013.

— Michael Sasges

List of Names

At least 6 of the 44 Great War soldiers remembered on the Merritt cenotaph are poorly remembered. No man with the surname of Beans, Tilamoose or Tommage ever served in the Canadian Expeditionary Force or Canadian Corps. No soldiers with the surnames of Connor or Patterson and forenames shortened to "J." ever acknowledged a Nicola Valley association on their attestation papers. Valley newspapers never recorded the lives or deaths of a Connor or Patterson. John McInulty's surname is misspelled.

YEAR OF DEATH: 1915

Birch, J.	McGee, J. C.
Davidson, R.	Wright, H. P.

YEAR OF DEATH: 1916

Barnes, B.	Fisher, H. G.	Scobie, J.
Baugh, J.	Jones, E. W.	Service, J.
Baxter, W.	McCoid, R.	Singleton, R. G.
Collins, G.	Mitchell, G.	Tilamoose [Charters], T.
Conner, J.	Murray, W.	Wilcox, J.
Cook, Leslie	Nash, J. F.	

YEAR OF DEATH: 1917

Berkeley, A. J.	Harrower, J.	Poole, S.
Bone, A.	Hogg, A. J.	Shuttleworth, A.
Bradley, W. L.	Hogg, D.	Thompson, W. P.
Busk, I.	Hynd, P.	
Cochenour, R.	McAulty [McInulty], J.	

YEAR OF DEATH: 1918

Drybrough, W.	Hobson, J. A.	Nicol, H.
Ferguson, R.	Lindsay, N.	Paul, J.

YEAR OF DEATH: 1919

King, F.

YEAR OF DEATH: UNKNOWN

Beans, T. H.	Patterson, J.
Connor, J.	Tommage, W.

Endnotes

1   At least 335 men from the Nicola Valley volunteered for Great War military service. A "roll of honour" in a valley church is the source of the count. The Nicola Valley Museum, when it published an alphabetized transcription of the roll, acknowledged the probability of omissions with these words: "We realize there are more names that could be added." "Nicola Valley Military Part Three," *Nicola Valley Historical Quarterly*, 1996. Neither the two women who volunteered for military service nor at least one man who was drafted in the last years of the war are named in the roll of honour.

2   The population of BC was almost 180,000 in the 1901 census year and almost 525,000 by 1921. Department of Trade and Commerce, *Sixth Census of Canada, 1921: Volume 1–Population*, 3-4, tables 1 and 3 (Ottawa, 1924), http://publications.gc.ca /collections/collection_2017/statcan/CS98-1921-1-1924.pdf. The population was almost evenly split between rural and urban residency in the 1901 and 1921 censuses (*Sixth Census*, 345, table 18). The pivotal urbanization experience occurred in the province's tidewater southwest. Vancouver's population was 27,010 in 1901, 100,401 in 1911 and 117,217 in 1921 (*Sixth Census*, 244, table 12). The provincial government incorporated at least 28 cities and towns in the first two decades of the twentieth century and 26 in the last three decades of the nineteenth. British Columbia Ministry of Communities, Sport and Cultural Development, "British Columbia Regional Districts, Municipalities, Corporate Name, Date of Incorporation and Postal Address." https://gov.bc.ca/assets/gov /british-columbians-our-governments/local-governments/finance /local-government-statistics/name_incorp_2014.xls. There were about 1,300 miles of railway track in 1900 and about 4,200 miles in 1919. Department of Agriculture, *The Statistical Year-Book of Canada*

for 1900 (Ottawa, 1901), 354. https://www66.statcan.gc.ca/eng/1901
-eng.htm. Department of Trade and Commerce, *The Canada Year
Book 1920* (Ottawa, 1921), 461. https://www66.statcan.gc.ca/eng
/1921-eng.htm.

3   The distances are computed from the latitudes and longitudes
of the mouth of the Fraser and the headwaters of the Nicola, and of
Merritt and Vancouver, as published on BC Geographical Names
(http://apps.gov.bc.ca/pub/bcgnws/). *Ecology of the Bunchgrass
Zone* is a BC government brochure available online at http://for.gov
.bc.ca/hfd/pubs/Docs/Bro/Bro54.htm.

4   "Horses were probably introduced to the Okanagan people
in the early 18th century by the Sanpoil, Columbia and Colville
tribes. In turn, the Okanagans traded horses with the Similkameen
and Thompson." Michael Blackstone and Rhonda McAllister, "First
Nations Perspectives on the Grasslands of the Interior of British
Columbia," *Journal of Ecological Anthropology* 8 (2004).

5   "Memories of Middlesboro: The Remembrances of Bertha Dell,"
Nicola Valley Archives Association, 2001.

6   James Teit, *The Thompson Indians of British Columbia* (1900),
(Merritt: Nicola Valley Museum Archives Association, 1997).

7   "Nicola," *Guide to the Province of British Columbia for the year
1877–78* (Victoria: T. N. Hibben, 1877), http://bccd.vpl.ca/index.php
/browse/title/1877-1878/Guide_to_the_Province_of_BC.

8   The *British Columbia Sessional Papers* published the electoral
counts originally. The University of BC has digitized the papers and
published them online at open.library.ubc.ca/collections/bcsessional.

9   The Geological Survey of Canada published two reports by
George Dawson on the Nicola Valley coal measures in 1878 and

1894. The GSC published a third report, by another scientist, R W. Ellis, in 1904. The provincial government published extracts in the *Annual Report of the Minister of Mines for the Year ending December 31st 1905 in the Province of British Columbia*, 1906 (cmscontent.nrs .gov.bc.ca/geoscience/PublicationCatalogue/AnnualReport/BCGS _AR1905.pdf).

10   The Thompson-Nicola Regional District Library System has digitized and shared all the *Merritt Herald* weeklies and predecessors from 1910 onward. (Nicola Valley Museum and Archives volunteers scanned the pages.) Online at arch.tnrl.ca.

The University of British Columbia's Historical Newspapers project has digitized and posted online all the extant issues of two other valley weeklies. Start here: http://open.library.ubc.ca/collections /bcnewspapers.

11   "Typical of pioneer industrialists in British Columbia, [John] Hendry brought technical skills from an earlier centre to the rich resources of the province. He was unusual in the scale of his success: he introduced 'big business' to the forest industry by creating an integrated company that controlled all aspects of production, distribution, and marketing:" *Dictionary of Canadian Biography*, s.v. "Hendry, John," by Jamie Morton, http://biographi.ca/en/bio/hendry _john_14E.html.

12   The Merritt Coalfield surrendered up 2.4 million tonnes of bituminous—or all-purpose—coal between 1906 and 1963: British Columbia Ministry of Mines and Energy, "Merritt Coalfield," (2004) http://gov.bc.ca/gov/content/industry/mineral.

Barrie Sanford, *McCulloch's Wonder: The Story of the Kettle Valley Railway* (1977; repr., North Vancouver: Whitecap Books, 2006) is the source for the cause and course of construction of the short line.

The City of Vancouver Archives' William McNeill fonds is a collection of correspondence between John Hendry and his personal secretary, William McNeill, which records Hendry's role in the arrival of coal mining in the Nicola Valley.

The Nicola Valley Coal and Coke prospectus and its statement of potential markets is online at http://archive.org/details /cihm_83343/page/n5.

13   *Annual Report of the Minister of Mines for the Year ending 31st December, 1912*, 280–288, http://cmscontent.nrs.gov.bc.ca /geoscience/PublicationCatalogue/AnnualReport/BCGS_AR1912 .pdf.

14   St. Andrew's Presbyterian and Wesley Methodist were built in Merritt in 1910 and St. Michael's Anglican two years later. All are extant, the chapel today a funeral parlour.

15   The Nicola Valley Museum's Merritt Volunteer Fire Department fonds has a copy of the department's minutes from 1911 onward.

16   Henry Standley Cleasby, *The Nicola Valley in Review* (Merritt: Merritt Herald, 1958). Nicola Valley Museum, "Interview with the Mayor," no date.

17   The United Church of Canada British Columbia Conference Archives/Bob Stewart Archives has custody of the records of Trinity United Church, Merritt, which includes the records of the predecessor Methodist churches and the minutes of meetings of the lay leadership.

18   Dominion of Canada, *Annual Report of the Department of Indian Affairs for the Year Ended June 30 1902* (Ottawa, 1902), 243, 249, http://bac-lac.gc.ca/eng/discover/aboriginal-heritage/first-nations /indian-affairs-annual-reports/Pages/item.aspx?IdNumber=15139.

Annual Report…for the Year Ended March 31 1912 (Ottawa, 1912), Part II, 12.

19   DIA *Annual Report…for the Year Ended March 31 1910*, 222.

20   John Chelahitsa's father was a leader of the Syilx people when the first settlers arrived in the Nicola Valley. His paternal great-uncle Wistesmetxe'qen (Walking Grizzly Bear), or Nkwala or N'kwala, was that Nicolas or Nicola after whom the river and its countryside were named.

John Tetlenitsa's portraits, songs and stories circulate online, an indicator of his importance and influence. The Chief Tetlenitsa Memorial Outdoor Theatre, at the confluence of the Nicola and the Thompson, is another. It opened in 2010, the centenary of the gathering of Indigenous leaders in Spences Bridge to prepare the statement they presented to Laurier.

Wendy Wickwire's entry (s.v. "Teit, James Alexander,") in the *Dictionary of Canadian Biography* is a succinct introduction to the life of the ethnographer and political activist (http://biographi.ca/en/bio/teit_james_alexander_1884_15E.html).

21   "To Sir Wilfrid Laurier, Premier of the Dominion of Canada/From the Chiefs of the Shuswap, Okanagan and Couteau [Thompson] Tribes of British Columbia/Presented at Kamloops, 25th August, 1910." *Teit Times: An Occasional Paper* (Merritt: Nicola Valley Museum and Archives Association, 1995).

22   The essential readings are Cole Harris, "Imposing a Solution, 1898-1938," in *Making Native Space* (Vancouver: UBC Press, 2002); Jean Barman, "Population Explosion, 1886-1914," and "Disregard of Native Peoples, 1858-1945," in *The West beyond the West: A History of British Columbia (Revised Edition)*, (Toronto: University of Toronto Press, 1991, 1999); and Allen Seager, "The Resource Economy,

1871–1921," in *Pacific Province*, ed. Hugh J. M. Johnston (Vancouver: Douglas and McIntyre, 1996).

23   The Canadian Virtual War Memorial (http://veterans.gc.ca /eng/remembrance/memorials/canadian-virtual-war-memorial) is the primary source for dates of death. The seven Books of Remembrance in the Peace Tower in Ottawa are the virtual memorial's source. Library and Archives Canada has digitized all the surviving Circumstances of Death cards, available online at http:// bac-lac.gc.ca/eng/discover/mass-digitized-archives/circumstances -death-registers/pages/circumstances-death-registers.aspx. They make for remarkable reading. Almost 60,000 Canadians died while soldiering (or nursing). LAC has also published the service folders of about 620,000 men and women who served in the Great War (http://bac-lac.gc.ca/eng/discover/military-heritage /first-world-war/personnel-records/Pages/search.aspx). Dates of death they record are occasionally wrong, but usually corrected.

24   One soldier at a machine gun could produce a rate of fire equal to 40 soldiers firing their rifles. John Keegan, *The Face of Battle: A Study of Agincourt, Waterloo and the Somme* (London: Jonathan Cape, 1976), 232. The lethality of artillery changed little in the three centuries after the first cannon appeared in the sixteenth century on Europe's battlefields, "Then, in the second half of the nineteenth century, there occurred a series of advances so brilliant as to render the artillery in use when the century closed probably 10 times as efficient as that which marked its opening." *Encyclopedia Britannica Online*, s.v. "Artillery." http://britannica.com/technology /artillery. Keegan writes that a French cannonball fired at a British grenadier or guardsman at Waterloo in 1815 would decapitate, amputate "or otherwise grossly mutilate the human frame" (*Face of Battle*, 269–270). A heavy German shell fired at a British trench in 1915 could make a soldier disappear. Explosions of artillery shells and bombs caused 70 per cent of Great War casualties, according to Keegan.

25   The BC Archives has published online two photographs of
the first train leaving Kamloops, C-03211, "BC Horse leave for
Valcartier, Quebec, Kamloops, Aug. 27, 1914," and C-03212, "BC
Horse leave for Valcartier, Quebec, Kamloops, Aug. 27, 1914." http://
search-bcarchives.royalbcmuseum.bc.ca/world-war-1914-1918
-mobilization.

26   G. W. L. Nicholson, C.D. *Official History of the Canadian Army
in the First World War*, (Ottawa: Ministry of National Defence, 1962),
31. As military achievement, the assembly and passage of the "first
contingent" of the Canadian Expeditionary Force was not without its
challenges, and Nicholson enumerates them.

27   The war museum's online illustrated commentaries and
observations about the use of gas in the Great War will appeal
equally to those who know nothing about the weapon and to those
who want to know more. Start at warmuseum.ca/firstworldwar/history
/battles-and-fighting/weapons-on-land/poison-gas/.

28   Library and Archives Canada had digitized the war diaries
of Canadian Expeditionary Force and Canadian Corps units and
formations at bac-lac.gc.ca/eng/discover/military-heritage/first-world
-war/Pages/war-diaries.aspx.

29   Andrew Godefroy, "Portrait of a Battalion Commander:
Lieutenant-Colonel George Stuart Tuxford at the Second Battle
of Ypres, April 1915," *Canadian Military Journal*, 2003. The article
published the colonel's report on Second Ypres, from which his
assessment of his men's circumstances on the morning of April 26
has been quoted.

30   Godefroy, "Tuxford," observes of the casualty rate: "Although
5th Battalion casualties were relatively light in comparison with other
Canadian infantry battalions engaged at the Second Battle of Ypres,
Tuxford's unit later suffered the brunt of casualties during difficult

fighting in the Battle at Festubert at the end of May. By the beginning of July, the 5th Battalion had received only enough reinforcements to bring the strength up to 698 men, nearly 300 less than its normal authorized strength."

31   The Canadian War Museum says that only mounted troops wore helmets before the Great War, and wore them mostly for show. The war museum's online illustrated commentaries and observations about Great War helmets (http://warmuseum.ca/firstworldwar /objects-and-photos/equipment-and-vehicles/uniforms-and-personal -gear/helmet/) are informative.

32   "Censorship," in the *International Encyclopedia of the First World War*, is a survey of the censorship efforts of all the major belligerents, and, equally, an unintended appreciation of the circulation of news from the front in the Nicola Valley.

33   "Menin Gate (Ypres) Memorial," Canadian Virtual War Memorial, http://veterans.gc.ca/eng/remembrance/memorials/canadian-virtual -war-memorial/cem?cemetery=91800.

34   Le Touret is one of 23,000 Commonwealth War Graves Commission cemeteries around the world. In these cemeteries are buried the remains of 1.7 million men and women killed in the First and Second World Wars.

35   "The Somme … is one of the most haunting place names in history—a small, marshy French river—synonymous now with misery and death. In the summer of 1916, around the Somme valley north of Paris, the British Army began one of the largest campaigns of the First World War. Five hellish months later, more than one million soldiers, including almost 25,000 Canadians and Newfoundlanders, had been killed or wounded in a series of battles that gained little for either side:" *The Canadian Encyclopedia*, s.v. "The Somme," http:// thecanadianencyclopedia.ca/en/article/the-somme-editorial.

36   The provincial government discouraged the pre-emption of Crown land to Indigenous buyers. It did not, however, prohibit Indigenous ownership of land.

37   Gilbert Malcolm Sproat, "Field Minutes," *Federal and Provincial Collections of Minutes of Decision, Correspondence, and Sketches.* Sproat's 1878 visit to the Nicola Valley established the valley's human geography that exists to this day. He was on Dominion and provincial government assignment, engaged in the allotment of reserves. The Union of BC Indian Chiefs has digitized Sproat's record of his allotments around the province and published them on its website (http://jirc.ubcic.bc.ca).

38   Sproat, "Field Minutes."

39   DIA, *Annual Report…for the Year Ended March 31, 1915,* 89, http://bac-lac.gc.ca/eng/discover/aboriginal-heritage/first-nations /indian-affairs-annual-reports/Pages/search.aspx.

40   Nina Woolliams, *Cattle Ranch: The Story of the Douglas Lake Cattle Company,* (Vancouver: Douglas & McIntyre, 1979).

41   Vimy Foundation, "The Battle at Vimy Ridge," http:// vimyfoundation.ca/the-battle-at-vimy-ridge. The purpose of the foundation is to "preserve and promote Canada's First World War legacy as symbolized with the victory at Vimy Ridge in April 1917, a milestone where Canada came of age and was then recognized on the world stage."

42   *The Canadian Encyclopedia,* s.v. "Battle of Vimy Ridge," http:// thecanadianencyclopedia.ca/en/article/vimy-ridge.

43   The First World War sacrifice was also a starting line for Canada's social-service and health-care programs. The "Welfare State" entry in *The Canadian Encyclopedia* (thecanadianencyclopedia.ca/en/article

/welfare-state) is an approachable primer on the contribution of the
war to the provision by government of social benefits and services
in Canada.

44   Byng was Governor General of Canada from 1921 to 1926.

45   Two histories written as the battle's centenary approached, Tim
Cook's *Vimy: The Battle and the Legend* and Ian McKay and Jamie
Swift's *The Vimy Trap*, consider the significance of the "birth of a
nation" status attributed to Vimy.

46   Crump: "1. A hard hit, given with brisk or abrupt effect. 2. The
explosion of a heavy shell or bomb, or the sound of this." *Oxford
English Dictionary Online*, s.v. "crump, n.4," http://www.oed.com
/view/Entry/45212?isAdvanced=false&result=3&rskey=1A8Mxn&.

47   The 72nd Battalion had been occupying Vimy Ridge trenches
off and on since Christmas Eve, 1916. "Wastage" was one source of
the battalion's diminished number on Easter Sunday. "Even in the
so-called quiet moments, trench life witnessed a steady trickle of
death and maiming," the Canadian War Museum reports. "Outside
of formal battles, snipers and shells regularly killed soldiers in
the trenches, a phenomenon known as 'wastage.'" Each month
10 per cent of a battalion's soldiers could be killed or wounded.
"Trench Routine," Canadian War Museum, https://warmuseum
.ca/firstworldwar/history/life-at-the-front/trench-conditions/trench
-routine. Two night raids, one of them using poison gas, were a
second source of the 72nd Battalion's diminished number.

48   "Perhaps the most important work leading up to the battle was
the secret construction of 11 tunnels or subways—totalling nearly
6 km in length—designed to bring many in the first wave of assaulting
troops safely out in front of the German lines, without having to
cross, under fire, a wide area of open ground or 'no man's land' at
the opening of the battle. Each subway was equipped with electric

lighting, water supplies, first aid stations and dug-out chambers for battalion headquarters staff." "Battle of Vimy Ridge," *The Canadian Encyclopedia*.

49   It was common for women to travel from Great Britain to Canada to join their husbands. On one immigrant ship, RMS *Empress of Britain*, the purser used a stamp, "GOING TO HUSBAND," to expedite preparation of the passenger lists required by Canadian law.

50   The *Victoria History of the County of Durham*, in preparation when the two Hogg households left the county for BC, asserts the influence of the north of England this way: from 1825 when a Stockton and Darlington steam locomotive first passed between colliery, tidewater and metropolitan London, "the construction of railways spread from the county of Durham over the whole kingdom, favouring the development of the coal trade, not only by the increased consumption of [the] fuel, but also by affording a means of cheap and easy transport for quantities of mineral which would have been practically impossible without their assistance. The locomotive engine and the railway may fairly be said to be the direct products of the north-country coal-trade."

51   The older David said he was a miner when he enlisted in December 1915. His mother said the younger David was a miner in the 1921 census.

52   The colliers of England's northeast were either on strike or locked out in 1810, 1825, 1831, 1832, 1844, 1849, 1863, 1879, 1887, 1891, 1892 and 1893 (at least): Robert Moore, *Pit-men, Preachers & Politics: The Effects of Methodism in a Durham Mining Community* (New York: Cambridge University Press, 1974). The dynamic pursuit of better living and working conditions is told, contemporaneously, in Richard Fynes, *The Miners of Northumberland and Durham: A History*

of their Social and Political Progress (Blyth, Northumberland: John Robinson, 1873), archive.org/details/minersnorthumbe00fynegoog.

53   Canada interned people from the German and Austrian empires during the First World War and Japanese Canadians and Japanese nationals during the Second World War.

54   "Address to the Members of the Merritt Branch & Auxiliary, by the Secretary F.J. Hogg on the evening of Feb. 5 1940" is on file in the office in the Legion's Nicola Valley branch.

55   "Robert Macnicol/Supervisor (BC)/Canadian Legion War Services to J.W. Langley/Canadian War Services' Drive/Merritt, BC Feb. 20 1940" is on file at the Legion's Nicola Valley branch.

56   Eric Brown and Tim Cook, "The 1936 Vimy Pilgrimage," Canadian War Museum, http://canadianmilitaryhistory.ca/wp-content/uploads/2012/03/5-Brown-and-Cook-Vimy-Pilgrimage-v-2.pdf

57   Barman, "British Columbia's Gentleman Farmers," in *History Today* 34 (1984), makes its subject the gentle pretensions of the orchardists of the Okanagan Valley before the Great War. Barman, *West beyond the West*, includes her appreciation of the influence of middle-class Britons.

58   Nash was probably exhausted on the day he died, tormented by lice and surrounded by rats, dead and alive. The Canadian War Museum entitles its online introduction to trench warfare "Rats, Lice, and Exhaustion."

59   Familysearch.org has published "British Columbia, Crown Land Pre-emption Registers, 1860–1971" on its website. The record of John Foster Paton Nash's pre-emption is in the Nicola register.

60   An outline life of James Okey Nash (1862–1943) is the source for these two paragraphs. In the fullness of his years, James Okey, BA Oxon '86, MA Oxon '89, was a headmaster and prelate in South Africa and the subject of a short *Times of London* obituary. His participation in a Church controversy and his leadership of a monastery after his return to the UK nominated him for inclusion in An Anglo-Catholic Congress Clergy Directory (http://anglicanhistory .org/england/congresses/blain_hickton2015.pdf). I confirmed the compilers' vital events information through the England and Wales censuses from 1841, published online through ancestry.ca.

61   There has been a post office at Quilchena since 1885.

62   *Dictionary of Canadian Biography*, s.v. "Guichon, Joseph," by John Douglas Belshaw, http://biographi.ca/en/bio/guichon_joseph _15E.html.

63   The BC government has published online the historic forest service annual reports at for.gov.bc.ca/hfd/pubs/docs/mr/annual /annualrpt.htm.

64   By the Great War the provincial government was managing the wildlife resource as a generator of provincial revenues, the BC Archives introduction to the game warden files notes, "through payment of licence fees, and international promotion of the province as a sportsperson's centre." The development of the province's game management policies and procedures is examined, absolutely and comparatively, in John Donihee, "The Evolution of Wildlife Law in Canada," Canadian Institute of Resources Law Occasional Paper 9 (Calgary: University of Calgary, 2000). One important Donihee observation: "The Canadian Constitution did not make explicit reference to wildlife or to game at the time of Confederation. Nevertheless extensive legislative powers with respect to wildlife are vested in the provinces and provincial ownership of public lands

confers both legislative and, arguably, proprietary interests with respect to wildlife in the provinces."

65   The Union of BC Indian Chiefs has published presentations to the commissioners on its Our Homes are Bleeding website.

66   The land and the water that ensured occupancy of the land were the Nicola Valley's foundational natural resources. Their use was, and is, largely regulated by the provincial government. The timber on the land and the mineral and energy (coal) resources beneath the land were, and are, also regulated by the provincial government. Regulation was historically fitful, less an activity of inspection and correction and more an activity of registration and exploitation.

67   "The age difference is of perennial interest with regular comment, both academic and popular, on the frequency, social acceptability and sociobiological basis for various age gaps between partners. The issue is of demographic interest because of its connection with the question of how the marriage market operates, and is of relevance for actuarial purposes and in a policy context also," Máire Ní Bhrolcháin, "The Age Difference at Marriage in England and Wales: A Century of Patterns and Trends," *Population Trends* 120 (2005): 7–14, http://semanticscholar.org/paper/The-age -difference-at-marriage-in-England-and-a-of-Bhrolch%C3%A1in /71be67a996dacfb515fb3da645900c5e9b2625fb.

Among Dr. Ní Bhrolcháin's observations: 1. The mean age difference in English and Welsh marriages, 1921 to 1901, is in the range of two to three years, but the range is "not in any sense typical. No more than a quarter of all marriages in a selection of years feature a gap of two to three years. 2."There is little evidence that the age gap in marriage is subject to strong social norms. Age differences appear to reflect, to a significant extent, the age distributions of people available for marriage."

A recent call for papers about the influence of the Great War on European marriage, divorce and gender relationships makes this observation about a marriage like the Nash-Wilson union: "Women marrying a partner much older than themselves had lower bargaining power than their counterparts who were married to a man of more or less the same or younger age. Regardless of where we ought to place the causes of changes, trends in the age differential between partners for the period 1900–1930 can shed light on gender dynamics within households."

68   The Women's Library, London School of Economics and Political Science, has custody of the records of at least five female-emigration organizations. The library's collection of essays on the emigration of British women starts in the 1970s.

69   The yearbooks are online on the Statistics Canada website at https://www65.statcan.gc.ca/acyb_r003-eng.htm.

70   At least one other woman from the Nicola Valley passed some or most of the Great War in the British Isles. Marie Flick's address, from 1916, was Deddington, near Banbury, Oxfordshire, according to her husband's service folder. She, like Eleanor Nash, was a native of the British Isles. The Canadian War Museum, responding to an inquiry from me, reports that travel to the UK by soldiers' spouses was common in the first years of the Great War, with the first restriction introduced in 1916 and a ban imposed in 1917. In the latter year Germany declared its submarines would attack any merchant vessel, enemy or neutral, that they might find in the coastal waters of the British Isles.

71   "Common affiliation with the Church of England, or [the] Anglican church, encouraged a feeling of superiority. As a woman put it as late as 1925, although personally she 'would greatly prefer Anglican to Presbyterian, on account of the beautiful

service, ...Anglicans often think they own the earth.'" Barman, "Population Explosion," *West beyond the West*, 141.

72   How Norman Lindsay endured the battlefields of Belgium and France for so long without losing his mind will never be known. If he ever said how, what he said has not survived. John Keegan offers insights into battle endurance in the two "Will to Combat" chapters in his *Face of Battle*. The "Reason in Madness" chapter of Modris Eksteins's *Rites of Spring: The Great War and the Birth of the Modern Age* (Toronto: Lester & Dennys, 1989) is another important analysis.

73   "Lindsay-Vaughan-Irving Family Tree," ancestry.ca.

74   A soldier from British Columbia, Lt. G. M. Flowerdew, received a posthumous Victoria Cross for leading a Strathcona's Horse cavalry charge in the spring of 1918, in France. The Canadian War Museum observes that mounted charges were rare: "Unable to break the trench deadlock and of little use at the front, cavalry remained behind the lines for much of the war."

75   *The Canadian Encyclopedia*. s.v. "Influenza (Flu)," http://thecanadianencyclopedia.ca/en/article/influenza.

76   Everett Sharp, "The Etaples Flu Pandemic?", http://ww1centenary.oucs.ox.ac.uk/body-and-mind/the-etaples-flu-pandemic/.

77   The All Saints' Parish (Shulus, BC) records are in the custody of the Anglican Provincial Synod of British Columbia Archives.

78   Each provincial police constable monthly submitted a four-page report to his supervisor. The BC Archives has custody of the reports.

79   Nancy Turner, Laurence Thompson, M. Terry Thompson and Annie York, "Thompson Plant Medicines Encountered in this Study,"

Thompson Ethnobotany: Knowledge and Usage of Plants by the Thompson Indians of British Columbia (Victoria: Royal BC Museum Publishing, 1990) 45, table 5.

80   Woolliams, *Cattle Ranch*, reports that the ranchers of the Nicola Valley, to demonstrate that their common lands, or commonages, were better used for grazing cattle than for cultivating grains and vegetables, in 1913 persuaded the provincial government to sponsor an unirrigated experimental farm in the high country. Grasshoppers ate "the entire year's work" in 1920 and ended the dry-farming experiment. The first of many expressions of the hope that an experimental farm in Nicola Valley might prove it could support grazing and growing appears in an April 8, 1910, *Merritt Herald and Nicola Valley Advocate* story about a meeting of the local Board of Trade. "Further correspondence respecting experimental fruit farms was also read but no assurance was forthcoming that one of these farms would be located in the Nicola Valley." The board later in the year entered apples from the valley in an apple show in Vancouver. " It is only a matter of three or four years when Nicola valley will be one of the finest fruit growing districts of BC," the December 16, 1910, *Herald* commented.

81   Barman, "In Search of British Columbia," *West beyond the West*.

82   Barman, "Population Explosion," *West beyond the West*, 359.

83   Harris, *Making Native Space*, 265, 266-267.

Index

Photographs indicated by page numbers in italics